Dude, The World's Gonna Punch You in the Face

Here's How to Make it Hurt Less

Dude, The World's Gonna Punch You in the Face

Here's How to Make it Hurt Less

Kris Wilder & Lawrence A. Kane
With Marc MacYoung
Illustrated by Mike Beery

Cover photo by Lawrence Kane

Illustrations by MSB Design, Seattle
(mike@msbdesign.net)

Cover design and interior layout by Kami Miller

Stickman Publications, Inc.
Burien, WA 98146
www.stickmanpublications.com

ISBN-13: 978-0692693490
ISBN-10: 0692693491

Disclaimer:

Information in this book is distributed "As Is," without warranty. Nothing in this document constitutes a legal opinion nor should any of its contents be treated as such. Neither the authors nor the publisher shall have any liability with respect to information contained herein. Further, neither the authors nor the publisher have any control over or assume any responsibility for websites or external resources referenced in this book. When it comes to martial arts, self-defense, violence, and related topics, no text, no matter how well written, can substitute for professional, hands-on instruction. These materials should be used *for academic study only.*

Praise for

Dude, The World's Gonna Punch You in the Face...

"1,700,000 people were murdered by the Khmer Rouge. I spent the first two years of my life in the Cambodian jungle running from them. I now have an accounting degree and a career with a leader in the logistics and distribution industry. The authors helped me get there. Now they've put it in a book for you. You should listen." – **Sophal Keo**, Senior Accountant.

"In a world of strikeouts, how you swing your bat makes all the difference. This book brings you to the plate of life strongly. Swing for the fences!" – **Mike Canonica**, Former Professional Umpire

"As an emergency room physician I see a lot of injuries. This book can save you a lot of pain and trauma, not just physical but also emotional and financial as well. Do yourself a favor, read it, and stay out of my Emergency Room." – **Jeff Cooper**, MD

"Finally a book that's not filled with psychological or sociological explanations or theories that nobody really wants to read. This book literally hits home. Things discussed here are the stuff of everyday life that every young person goes through which you won't find in any textbook. It is a must read if you want to be informed about which direction in life to take." – **David A. Davies**, Security Consultant and Author

"Growing old is not for sissies and the lessons Kane and Wilder put forward do not always come easily. We all wish we could have had (and listened too) this advice as we were growing up." – **John Lytle**, Sr. Business Executive

Table of Contents

Leadership

Work

Relationships

LIFE

VIOLENCE

Introduction

> "That is the greatest fallacy, the wisdom of old men. They do not grow wise. They grow careful."
>
> — Ernest Hemingway (1899 - 1961)

One stupid mistake ruined his life… Or, maybe it was a series of small missteps and one big betrayal?

~~~~~

As an 18-year-old college freshman he went on his first road trip to see a football game, travelling from Eugene, Oregon to Seattle, Washington. He'd never been out of state before so he was very excited. On the bus ride he experienced his first champagne brunch too, knocking back mimosas (orange juice mixed with champagne) along with his buddies. It was a party, and a good party at that. He never actually made it into the stadium though, *things went a little sideways…*
~~~~~

You see, he'd didn't realize how much he'd had to drink since mimosas don't taste much like alcohol. And, he'd never had any kind of adult beverage before so he didn't know how to hold his liquor. *He passed out in line* just outside the stadium's entrance gate. His buddies, set on seeing the game, dragged him over to the first aid room, dumped him there, and left.

At halftime the first aid crew sought out the freshman's friends. He was not allowed to remain in the first aid stand any longer, but they were given the opportunity to carry him back to the bus as long as someone was willing to stay with him while he slept it off to make sure that he didn't drown in his own puke. Sadly, no one was *willing to miss the game.*

~~~~~

This guy, a naïve college freshman 285 miles from home, woke up with a savage hangover. His friends were nowhere to be found. And, he discovered that he was in detox, a county run facility designed to keep addicts medically stable and safe during withdrawal. The hangover hurt badly enough, but that was just the beginning…

The pain went from bad to worse when Seattle PD officers *slapped him in handcuffs* and carted him off to *jail* where he found himself charged with minor-in-possession, public drunkenness, and a host of petty violations. He was also handed a bill for the ambulance ride, medical treatments, his stay in jail (he was booked Saturday night but couldn't see a magistrate until the courts opened on Monday morning), and a second one later on for attorney fees once his case was adjudicated.
~~~~~

On top of that he had to call his parents, explain why he'd missed the bus ride back to school, and beg his dad to skip work, travel to Seattle, pick him up, bail him out, and drive him back to Oregon.

All-in-all it was a $12,900 weekend. And, when his school discovered what he had done it cost him his scholarship too (there are conditions on scholarships and these include following the student code of conduct). So, on top of the $12,900 in fees for the experience, add four years of lost tuition and housing assistance at about $25,500 per year and that *one event cost this poor guy $114,900* and change.

Now let's throw in a blow to his self-respect, his family's regard, and his future and instead of a fun road trip we have the makings of a horrible, terrible, really bad day.

We all make mistakes, that's a basic part of the human condition, but this poor guy's momentary lapse of judgment compounded by his friends' betrayal was more impactful than most. However, even though everything that happened to him wasn't *fair*, it was *right*. It was legal and correct. And, it was *disproportionate*.

The world beat this young man down pretty good, but eventually he bounced back. He moved to another school and worked two jobs while struggling to complete his education, built up a pile of debt in lieu of scholarships, and took *seven years* to graduate. He overcame his criminal record and landed a decent job at a major corporation too. And, he is now on a path toward promotions.

Yes, he absolutely bounced back. But, he did it all *the hard way…*

~~~~~

We'd like to think that most of us aspire to use our time on earth wisely, do the right things, and leave behind a legacy that we can be proud of. Unfortunately, there are a host of hidden pitfalls that we must navigate along the way. Most young men *acquire wisdom* through *failure* and *pain* like that college freshman did, but it really doesn't *have* to be like that.

What if you were *warned about the dangers*—and possibilities—ahead of time? That is where this book comes in, it teaches you how to man-up and take on whatever the world throws at you. It arms young men with knowledge to augment their limited experience in vital subjects like love, wealth, education, faith, government, leadership, work, relationships, life, and violence. It won't prevent all mistakes, nothing will, but it can keep you from making the impactful ones that you'll *regret* the most.

You see, we only get one shot at life. And, as that college freshman discovered the hard way, it's really easy to screw that up. What can be done? Read on. Learn how to *see the bad things coming*, avoid them, and *set yourself up to be a success.*
~~~~~

How to use this book

"Knowledge speaks, but wisdom listens."

– Jimi Hendrix (1942 – 1970)

Hey! *Listen up*!

This book is written by guys for guys—no candy coating, no puff, just straight facts and crucial information that you need to know.

First off, we understand that you're probably not going to listen; we didn't. We may no longer have the attention spans of caffeine-addled, hyper manic lab rats, but we were your age once and we remember. We have kids your age too. So, it's likely that you will not listen. Not listening really isn't an age thing or even a generational thing, however, it is about the Y-chromosome. You are a guy, with a genetic predisposition *not* to listen all that well, at least not during your formative years.

As guys we like to do stuff, not spend our time with cerebral things like reading books. Sometimes, however, information does manage to make it through our thick skulls and land in a place where we can use it to our benefit. That knowledge may keep us out of *jail*, assure that our bones remain *intact*, keep our blood on the inside where it *belongs*, and assure that we will still have a full count of fingers and toes at the end of each work day.

So, you likely don't *want* to listen, but really *need* to.

This will make it easier: *Don't read this book from front to back*. It won't stick.

Put this book on the nightstand next to your bed, on the back of the toilet, on the armrest of your favorite chair, anyplace where you can take 30 seconds or a minute-and-a-half to *read the random page you flip it open to*. The order is not important unless you *want* it to be, because all the information you'll read in here stands alone and is immediately useful. Bam! No preparation beyond what you've already read in the introduction.

Do this: Read a short section, take the action listed at the bottom of the page, and feel the achievement.

You can thank us later.

MAN-UP

"If you can keep your wits about you while all others are losing theirs and blaming you, the world will be yours and everything in it. What's more, you'll be a man."

— Rudyard Kipling (1865 – 1936)

First, respect yourself

There's a lot of talk about respect and dignity these days, "You gotta respect me," "You don't respect me enough," "You need to pay respects," and so forth. Sure, we all want respect, *crave* it in fact, but more important than anything other people do, you need to respect yourself first. Without self-respect no one will ever respect you. That means that you've established lines of behavior that you simply will not cross, a code of ethics where you know with certainty what is acceptable and unacceptable to you. That takes introspection. You have to sit down and determine where your boundaries are. This doesn't mean being arrogant. It doesn't mean being rude. It simply means having a working internal *compass* that helps you *navigate* your life mentally, physically, and spiritually. In this fashion you will know where your lines are drawn, what you are willing to do, and most importantly what you are *not* willing to do. The content of your character is your *choice*, choose wisely.

Make a note of this: Many people demand respect and yet don't make the effort to earn it within themselves first. Reverse that common formula, *earn* your own respect first. As a man of *principle* your true character will shine through… and *that* is worthy of respect.

Stop being a little snowflake

The world isn't fair, it really can be brutal, but that doesn't mean that you should play the *victim*. Get tough. Stop walking around looking for your "safe space." Stop being offended by this, that, and the other thing. Nobody cares if you are offended outside of your family or close knit circle of friends, and maybe not even them despite the nice noises they make. Seriously, anybody else who says that they care is likely being paid to care by the government or some community service organization. Just move on, make a note, and live your life. Spending one second of thought or effort to be offended, threatened, or *irrationally* feel unsafe is a waste of time and energy. It means that somebody else has *rent-free space* in *your head*. It means that you're stuck, awkwardly living in the past. Further, quit looking to authority figures to do your "justified" dirty work. Learn how to put on your big boy pants and deal with your own problems all by yourself... or don't. The call is yours to make, but make it knowing that in order to be successful, to be a *real* man, you need to be able to handle things *yourself*. If you are hearing us, you are on your way to manhood, if you are rejecting what we say, well we would wish you good luck, but you wouldn't know what to do with it.

Hey, listen up: This is not about being macho, it is about being an adult. Start to live out your life as an adult. It's a journey. You don't have to do it all at once, just *move in the right direction* one day at a time. The alternative is to live out your life as a child, and that is a sad and pathetic thing.

Nobody cares about your happiness more than you

If you are sad your friends and family will try to help you, to intervene in some way to get you out of your funk. That's what friends do. The fact of the matter, however, is that nobody *can* or *should* care more about your mental health and happiness than you do. Now that doesn't mean that if things get bad, you shouldn't seek help. Quite the opposite, actually... Recognize if you have an issue that you are *unable* to deal with; that's the time to seek help from those around you. That could include classmates, coworkers, or clergy, but in some instances that may mean seeking professional help too. There is no shame in doing it. You go to a mechanic when your car isn't running correctly, right? You let the mechanic find the problem and resolve it. You go to a medical doctor for illnesses and injuries, right? Psychologists, psychiatrists, and others in the mental health profession do exactly the *same* thing if something's not working right in your brain. That's not a disparagement in any way, it's a medical *fact*. Throughout your adolescence your brain changes significantly. In many key ways it doesn't even *look* like an adult's brain until you've reached your early 20s. So if you are not doing well, and friends and family or a change in your routine is not making a difference, go ahead and contact a pro. It's the smart thing to do.

Bet you didn't know: All colleges and universities in the United States have free mental health facilities. And, psychiatric care is covered by all insurance plans. You're already paying for it, so why not take advantage of it if you need to?

Crying is not for the weak

An overabundance of joy can bring a person to tears, but more often than not tears result from extreme sorrow. Crying is a *normal* emotion, even tough guys *can* cry from time to time, but being a crybaby is a totally different thing. Crybabies are weak. They use whining, fit-throwing, and waterworks to get their way. It is the last, desperate action of a *losing* position. You see, crybabies learn early in life that throwing a tantrum is an effective way to get what they want and have immaturely carried that *childish* behavior into their adolescent years or beyond. The follow-up to a crybaby not getting his or her way is the pout, or sulk, which is nothing more than doubling-down on weak, childlike behavior. *Don't be a crybaby*. Not one male icon throughout history has ever been a crybaby, not a single one. Think about it… politicians, businessmen, and athletes who act like crybabies are held in distain, often teased or shunned by their relations for their immaturity. It takes a tough guy to shed a tear at a funeral or cry over another's tragedy, yet it is only immature wimps who cry all the time.

Think about it: Do you cry, pout, break things, or throw a fit when you don't get your way? We hope not. If you find any part of crybaby tendency in your life it will hold you back, make you less of a man. Hunt that weakness down and *kill* it right now.

Don't compare with envy

Shakespeare described envy as "the green sickness." Christians consider it a deadly sin (one that destroys the life of grace and charity within a person). Similarly, Buddha said, "He who envies others does not achieve peace." That's a pretty powerful message from a variety of different sources and perspectives, and one with which we should all agree. Coveting another person's possessions, relationships, or attributes does you absolutely no good whatsoever. Comparing yourself against others with envy is *ugly* and it looks really bad on you. If you are comparing yourself with others as a measure of where you would like to be or attributes you would like to obtain, however, that can be a *good* thing. In another's positive example you can *learn* how to achieve your own goals. In the business world we call this "benchmarking." Benchmarking can be a powerful learning experience as you discover and adopt proven practices rather than reinventing the proverbial wheel on your own. So, talk to mentors and coaches to compare, measure, and adopt successful ways. That is a fine thing. It is very important that you do so *without* envy, however. Envy distorts the picture.

The difference maker: Find somebody you look up to and identify one thing he or she does that you especially admire. Now, find a way to adopt that one thing into your life too.

Feeling sorry for yourself

It is not uncommon to feel sorry for yourself from time to time. To be focused inwardly on your problem, your conundrum, we are all guilty of it from time to time. It is a fundamental element of human existence to focus on the negative, but frankly that is behavior that comes from the bottom of the list. These self-pitying emotions stem from the lower levels of life and you need to *guard against* them, outright exterminate them whenever possible. A pity party is completely self-centered, leading you to wallow in misery, sorrow, and what-if thinking. It makes you *weak*. But, you don't have to be weak. If you find yourself depressed, feeling sorry for yourself, do a little introspection to discover the root cause. Then, figure out what *responsible* and *forward-moving* act will take you away from the bad place you're in and lead you to something *better*. Self-pity is only okay if it's short-lived and spurs you to positive action.

Kill it now: The immediate cure for feeling sorry for yourself is to get up and do something *for somebody else*. That's often called *servant leadership*, because in identifying and meeting the needs of their colleagues, communities, customers, or classmates, people can find higher value in themselves. It's really just that simple. Try it.

Complaining

The term "complaint" has a negative association attached to it, and it should as it is used today. Knowing what you need to have done to resolve an issue is an *effective* form of complaint however, it can flip a negative into a positive by delivering results. For example, if the guy in the theater in front of you is texting or talking on his phone during the movie, asking a theater employee to quiet him is a good thing. It removes the problem and simultaneously keeps you out of an unnecessarily confrontation so it's not an abrogation of your responsibility but rather enablement of the theater employee's job. They're pretty good at getting folks to shut up and watch the movie without annoying their neighbors because they have to do that sort of thing every day. Not knowing what you need to have happen, or what an effective alternative to your first resolution might be however, well that's *just complaining*. Complaining that it's raining outside, there's nothing good on TV, or that your favorite celebrity didn't win an Oscar this year, that sort of thing turns into a negative stream of garbage that nobody likes to be around. We like winners, not whiners. So, if you're going to complain only do it when you can get results to *change* a situation for the better.

Basic rules: Only complain when you are looking for an action. A pleasant and respectful complaint that stirs *positive* acts is a good thing. Complaining just to complain, however, is *worthless*. It makes you look whiny and weak.

Don't worry

Don't worry?! Boy, that's a hard one isn't it? A few years ago Kris watched a man who was running for the United States Congress in a heated competition. On election night the candidate looked at his staffers who were focused on the close returns and declared, "The votes are cast. It's just the counting that needs to be done. The wife and I are going to go up to our hotel room to get some rest. We'll see you in the morning." And, that is exactly what he did. It was an amazing display of *not* worrying. Take a moment to consider the last thing you worried about. Did worrying *change* the outcome in any way whatsoever? Nope, not one iota… The concern and the help needed to address that concern are different emotions and actions. Worry has no *action* attached to it, and action does *not* need worry in order to be effective. In fact, worry is not needed for any action or emotion. We all need to learn from the past and plan for the future, that's constructive, but worry is ineffectual. Worry is worthless. Flush it. By focusing on *actions* you can transform worthless worry into something positive. That flips the equation and makes it worthwhile.

Try this: When you find your mind spinning, thinking only of the "woulda," "coulda," "shouldas," that's the time to *break* the cycle. Ignore your worries and focus on the actions, the things you can actually do something about. Take a piece of paper or fire up your tablet and jot down what you *want*. From that intended outcome, work backwards listing all the things you can *do* directly or indirectly (by influencing others to take actions on your behalf) to make the problem or opportunity work out the way you would like it to. Now, *quit worrying* and take the *actions* that you've listed.

It isn't about you

Have you noticed that when you're driving a car your whole world becomes all about the vehicle you're riding in? Bicyclists and pedestrians are a nuisance when they interrupt your commute, right? But, if you're riding a bike or walking down the street it's the cars that get in your way that are annoying. The world has not changed, yet your *perspective* changes everything. Similarly, it's easy to be offended by the actions of others, but more often than not whatever they've done to piss you off was *not* intentional. They are busy trying to satisfy their own needs, to get what they want done, and likely never even consider or notice their impact on *you*. This means it's *not personal.* Nobody ever got up in the morning and said, "I'm going to go seek you out and purposely cut you off in traffic just to ruin your day." It is highly unlikely that your roommates, neighbors, the cops, or your friends, relatives, boss, or teachers *actually* have it in for you. Even when folks don't like you, they have better things to do than plot some grand, Illuminati-type conspiracy against you and your interests. The world really isn't trying to ruin your day. While it may feel that way, it truly isn't all about you.

Your smart move: The more you realize that what happens isn't about you, the easier life becomes. Don't take things personally.

Big rocks

If you've already heard this story, bear with us. It's important… A professor stood in front of his class with a big jar and placed a dozen rocks inside, filling it to the top. He asked, "Is this jar full?" When the students said that it was he replied, "Really?!" Then, he poured in some gravel and shook the jar causing the small rocks to work themselves down into the spaces between the bigger ones. Once again he asked, "Is the jar full?" By this time the class was onto him, "Probably not," they replied. He nodded sagely and poured in some sand which settled into the spaces left between the rocks and gravel when he shook the jar once again. Once more he asked, "Is the jar full?" "No," the students replied. Nodding, he poured water into the jar until it was filled to the brim and asked, "What is the point of this illustration?" "No matter how full you think your schedule is, you can always fit more in?" a student guessed. "No," the professor replied. "The point is that if you don't put the big rocks in *first*, you'll never fit *everything* in."

Ponder this: There are only twenty four hours in the day and most of us sleep at least a third of that time, so we need to *prioritize*. What are the big rocks in your life? Is it preparing for a test that will make your GPA, completing a critical project at work, spending time with your family, hanging with your friends, traveling to see the world, reconnecting on social media, playing a newly released videogame, or something completely different that's most *important*? Knowing your priorities helps you make the best use of your time.

Old toys

Have you ever discovered an old toy in the attic, a memory box, or a storeroom, one you spent hours playing with as a child? It is a great sensation to find something you once loved isn't it? You might even amuse yourself with it for a moment to relive some good memories, but eventually you set it down and put it away again. The reason for this is that the toy comes from a *different* time in your life, it would look very odd for you to still be playing with it today. Other things in your life likely exist from this historical place as well. These might include childhood emotions, eating habits, or clothing choices by way of example, but there could be many, many more. What old "toys" are you carrying with you at this very moment? Have you taken an *audit* of yourself? If not, you should. Understand that there are times in life and certain things that are right for each time. Imagine if you will a grown man playing with his baby rattle, pacifier, or mobile on a daily basis. Pretty weird, huh? That's not all that much different from a hoarder who cannot throw anything away or an 80-year-old who insists on dressing and speaking like a teenager. Don't be the weird guy.

Let it go: There is an old saying, "If you love something let it go. If it comes back it was meant to be; if it doesn't then it never was." Some things just need to be let go. Don't clutter your life with old toys.

Love

"Love is an act of endless forgiveness, a tender look which becomes a habit."

— Peter Ustinov (1921 – 2004)

You can't fix crazy

A good rule of thumb is to *never* date anyone crazier than yourself. That's an amusing quip, but there's a scary truth lurking beneath the humor of it. If you are involved with a crazy girlfriend (or boyfriend for that matter), you need to leave *now*. Break it off. Don't see her anymore. You are *not* equipped to help her. You can't love her out of it. There are professionals with advanced educations and years of clinical experience who can't solve crazy. Think of all the people who are mentally ill yet refuse to take their medications, who voluntarily live on the streets, or who commit horrific crimes like spree shootings or cannibalism and you get a snippet of the fact that there are some personalities that simply *cannot be fixed*, even by professionals. And guess what, you have none of that training, none of that experience; it is simply not something that *you* can do. Don't live with rage, threats, intimidation, or abuse. Escape the land of crazy or abusive girlfriend right now.

Hey, listen up: Before getting engaged or married to someone you love, it's a very good idea to live together for *at least* a year. After all, it's relatively easy to be on your best behavior, to fake your way through a relationship while casually dating, but virtually impossible to do so when you're together all the time. That's when true character is uncovered. Better to know *before* you tie the knot than afterward when shattered feelings turn into expensive legal proceedings, and a host of other nasty complications arise.

Don't marry young

Statistics show that marrying young is likely to end in divorce. The fact of the matter is that people are always changing, evolving, and growing, it is just the way things are. Now the core of a person tends to stay pretty much the same, as closely held values are unlikely to change overmuch, but most folks become more mature and discover that their preferences and predilections change with time. Your late teens and early twenties are a particularly dynamic period in your life, the world is pushing on you and you are pushing back on it, *finding your way*. Many facets of a person's character, interests, and experience will *change* rapidly during this time. So, you need to know yourself, know your partner, and know that your partner knows herself (or himself) before you should ever *consider* getting married. Be prudent. Wait until you're *at least* 25 years of age, have finished school, and have settled into your career before you tie the knot. No matter how much you think you are in love and cannot wait, love is a really lousy reason to get married. To clarify, love is good, but it cannot be the *only* reason to marry, in part because most folks can't tell the difference between love, lust, and infatuation. Look toward deeper aspects of compatibility. For example, discuss things like how you make important decisions, handle money, approach spiritualism, or intend to raise children. A common and *compatible* worldview makes life much easier if you expect to spend the rest of it blissfully joined at the hip with someone else.

Try this: Unless it's for religious reasons or to raise children there's really no imperative to get married nowadays. If you think you've found the right person and that now is the time, go ahead and get *engaged*, but make the engagement *at least* a year long. Seriously one year or more. Long engagements are great tests. They help you be *sure* you're sure.

She will tell you, but you need to be able to hear

Every woman will tell you about herself. She will tell you what she values and what she doesn't value, you just have to listen. She will also send out warning signs, subtle indictors that should get your attention. For instance, you may hear "I made dinner plans for us tonight," but more than likely what you are *actually* hearing is a warning about the special occasion that merited those plans which you may have forgotten about. These seemingly casual conversations bring with them soft warnings, admonishments about behaviors, associations, or actions that you *need* to be aware of. If you listen carefully enough woman will also tell you if they are broken, how their history has made them into the person who is standing before you today. A comment like, "I have friends who live on the edge," "I don't like to be touched," or "I've been divorced three times" should really get your attention.

Understand *that* is only the tip of the iceberg. There is more to her story, frankly more than you really need to know about or get associated with. In a situation like that you need to leave.

Action tip: Body language is an inexact science. For instance, no single signal is a reliable indicator of truthfulness, physical attraction, or warning. Nevertheless, if you understand *how* to interpret signals that *consistently* support particular conclusions about what others are *actually* communicating when they speak it can help you succeed in life. It can even become a *survival skill* when you run across the wrong person or enter into the wrong relationship. Take a class, do Google search, or read a book, but however you acquire the competency it is vital to learn how to understand the subtle messages you're been missing. They come from everyone around you all the time.

You can't save her

People make choices and sometimes those choices are bad. A series of bad choices can easily cascade, building on top of each another until they culminate in a grand moment of, "Holy crap, how did I wind up here." Skipping a class, for instance, becomes skipping classes. Skipping classes leads to lower grades, lost opportunities, a subpar education, and a lifelong struggle to make ends meet. Similarly, recreational drug use *could* be relatively harmless, yet it often leads to poor associations. Poor associations, in turn, lead to bad environments where being in the wrong place at the right time turns into victimization and tragedy. Or addiction and all the vulnerabilities that come with it... It doesn't matter how smart or educated you are, if you make *enough* bad choices things simply *won't end well*. Consequently, if a woman (or man) you care about is on that path, living in that downward spiraling world, don't try to play knight-in-shining-armor and ride in to *fix* the situation. You don't have the training or experience to do it right. If she wants help, recognizes the error of her ways, and is taking positive actions on her own accord to climb up and out of the hole that she's dug for herself then take that into consideration, but people truly need to *want* to change in order to have any chance of succeeding. Even then, if they've fallen far enough or fast enough it's damnably hard to recover.

Codependence is not your friend: Well-intentioned people often *make things worse* by unwittingly being the safety net that supports their loved one's bad behaviors. If you think that your situation is different, special, or that you can break the cycle, you're wrong. It's not different, it is not special or unique, and you can't save her on your own. You *can* connect her with professionals in the community who may be able help, but you *can't* play the hero and expect to prevail. Don't even try.

Character always trumps looks

We all know beautiful people who know that they are good looking and play off of it to their advantage. That's all well and good, but the challenge is that those looks are not going to last forever. Consider how you perceive an A-List actress from a decade or two ago and think, "Wow she got *old*." Yes, we all do eventually. People get old. Life is fleeting. Looks fade. It's inescapable, over time we all let our bellies fall so to speak. Character, on the other hand, is enduring. Integrity is forever… or at least for a lifetime. And, it's a *choice*, a binary one. You either have it or you don't. Do you take the easy way out, lying, cheating, or stealing your way to success, or do you do the right thing even when no one else is looking? For those who choose that higher road, who follow a code of personal integrity and honor, that is something that you can utilize all of your life, something that never, ever gets old, gray, limping, or forgetful. Character is for keeps.

Jot it down: Pretend you're writing your obituary. How would you want to be remembered? *Write it down* and reflect back on it from time-to-time to make sure that you are *on the right path*. If you find yourself feeling down, out of sorts, or just generally disconcerted chances are good that it's your subconscious warning you that you've lost your way.

You don't have to win every argument

Arguments are not conversations, nor are they free exchanges of ideas. In fact, arguments are nothing more than one *ego* pitted against another ego with an intent to *win*. A "win" in this instance is defined as a having the other person succumb, to give-up and agree, or for you to get the last word in edgewise before the other guy (or gal) stomps off in a huff. Winning an argument may feel nice, but it is a pyrrhic victory (meaning that winning inflicts such a devastating toll on the victor that it is tantamount to defeat). It never holds over the long run since nothing is actually resolved and the other person *still disagrees* with your position. Consequently, the real result of winning is *animosity* more often than not. If that was your goal all along that's fine, but chances are good it's *not* the outcome you were looking for. In those instances it is okay to let it go, to *not win*, especially if it's *just* your ego that's involved. Sometimes the subject of the argument is a truly big deal, something that violates your core beliefs, and that's the time to *fight*. Most of the time, however, you're better off being the cool one, the calm one, knowing that a short-lived victory may ultimately cost you a longer term friendship or more. Sometimes it's even worthwhile to apologize when you've done nothing wrong simply to tamp down the drama or save the relationship, yet it takes a great deal of maturity to be able to know when it's the right approach and then actually do it in the heat of the moment.

Your smart move: The goal of the argument is often *clouded* by the emotion of the moment. If you're able to set that aside and focus on the underlying disagreement oftentimes you can turn the conversation into a discussion rather than letting it devolve into an argument. Keep the endgame in mind so that your *emotions* won't *overrule* your self-control, and be prepared to table (set aside) things for a while, let tempers cool, and readdress the issue later on.

The scariest—or greatest—word in the English language... "Pregnancy"

We're not going to admonish against premarital sex, and frankly children can be the greatest blessing in your life, but it's imperative to *know* that if you *accidentally* get a girl pregnant you will be at the mercy of whatever *she* chooses afterward. If you want to keep the child, she may choose to get an abortion, and you have nothing to say. If she decides to give the child up for adoption you have nothing to say. If she decides to keep the child you have nothing to say. But, if she does decide to keep the child, you are now on the hook for the child support (and, depending on your circumstances, where you live, and how good your attorney is taking care of her financial needs as well). Don't want to pay? Can't pay? The courts don't care—you *pay* either way. Your wages will be garnished (which means that your employer, complying with a court order, must deduct the money you owe directly from your paycheck before you ever see it). And, you really don't get to choose how much you will pay either; in most cases the courts decide. Further, there are no restrictions on how she spends the money, it is completely and totally her call. You turn over the court-determined amount of money every month until the child turns 18 years old, and even then your obligations might not be complete. Think you can say, "Whatever, I'm not paying!" Don't pay and guess what, the authorities will find you. If you owe enough back child support, the state will take away your passport and for good measure your driver's license too. And, all back child support must be paid in full before you can get your license back.

Heed the warning: Contraception is your friend. Until you *want* to have a child, until you're happily married or otherwise certain of your future, never let a few minutes of fun lead to an unwanted pregnancy that will change your whole life.

Divorce

Divorce is awful… and awful common nowadays. In fact according to divorcerate.org 50% of first marriages, 67% of second marriages, and 74% of third marriages in the United States end in divorce. It's a thriving industry. The challenge is that divorce is extraordinarily expensive, not just in money but in time and emotion too. And, it is the equivalent of a nuclear blast to any children who may be involved as well. Divorce should be an absolute *last* resort, something you undertake only in an abusive relationship or where truly irreconcilable differences prevail, ones you cannot ameliorate even after professional counseling. Understand that more often than not when love devolves into hatred it becomes a *war* that nobody wins, and it never ends if children are involved. In fact, there's an old adage that goes, "A divorce is never final until the last child dies." Scary, huh? It should be.

The difference maker: Lust is a thin veneer that wears off quickly, yet more often than not true love prevails. One way to tell if you really love somebody is that you feel a deep-seated desire to put *their welfare* ahead of your own, much like good parents do for their children. When that's your partner's mindset as well as your own common causes of divorce like sex and money become far less problematic. You seek compromise and resolution not so much for yourself as for your significant other. And *that* is a good thing.

Forgiving yourself

We all do stupid things from time to time, and we all have regrets. Regrets are a form of worry. They create a sense of sadness, strong emotions over things that likely cannot be fixed because it's *too late* to do so. In some instances we may get a second chance, but let's face it, second chances are few and far between. Sometimes we actually *want* our words or actions to *harm* others, yet most times we fail to anticipate the import of our actions until we belatedly discover what we've done. If you did something stupid on purpose you need to live with that shame, yet if it was done unintentionally you need to learn how to *forgive* yourself and move on. Let the emotion go, but not the lessons. It is kind of like gutting a fish, you throw away the useless viscera but keep the valuable flesh for your dinner. Forgiving yourself is just like that, throw away the junk and keep what's important. In this fashion regret is transformed from a harmful emotion to an impetus that spurs your personal growth.

Gut the fish: Take a regret, find the emotion, and let it go while keeping the vital lesson firmly in mind. Use that example to *safeguard* your future. Promise yourself that, "The next time [moment] happens, I am going to do [action]." In this fashion you can more easily live with your regrets.

Snakebites and letting it go

There is an old saying, "You don't die from the snakebite, you die from the poison," and it's true. The inability to forgive, to let go of something bad that has happened to you, is *poison*. It will eat away at your life. Now we are not suggesting that forgiveness is a simple or easy thing to do. In some instances the violation is so severe and so damaging that professional help is needed to compartmentalize, let it go, and move on. However, most of the time we face small- to middle-sized issues that *require* us to forgive, forget, and get on with our lives. It may take a little time, and it will require active work on your part, but forgiveness is *necessary* for a good life. Ever major religion has the tenant of forgiveness somewhere in its laws or rules. Journalist Joan Lunden (1950 -) once wrote, "Holding on to anger, resentment, and hurt only gives you tense muscles, a headache, and a sore jaw from clenching your teeth. Forgiveness gives you back the laughter and the lightness in your life." Listen to the wisdom of the sages, old and new, and don't let the poison of a snakebite make your blood bitter. Life is a lot brighter when you are *not* angry or resentful.

Make a note of this: When someone you care about hurts you, you have two choices: (1) You can *cling to resentment*, thoughts of revenge and retribution, or (2) you can *embrace forgiveness* and move on. If you're stuck that's likely your ego talking, not your common sense. It often helps to consider the situation from the other person's perspective, perhaps you would have acted similarly had you perceived things the same? And, think about times when you have intentionally or unintentionally hurt others who were bighearted enough to forgive *you*. If it's still a challenge to let things go, talk to an impartial third party such as a mentor, spiritual advisor, or counselor who can help you see the situation from a different perspective.

Secret relationships are a bad idea

If you need to keep your relationship a secret, hide it from your friends or family, it is a bad association. There's something embarrassing going on, something you're not proud of. Or, you're going behind another person's back in a *subversive or illicit* way. Perhaps you're being used or abused, or maybe it's simply not an affiliation of equals, but if you're uncomfortable enough that you feel the need to keep things secret then chances are good that you are *not* in a healthy situation. Healthy relationships require *mutual* respect, trust, honesty, support, equality, good communication, separate identities, and a sense of light-heartedness. This holds true with family members, friendships, coworkers, and romantic involvements alike. Unhealthy relationships, on the other hand often involve intimidation or threats, physical, economic, or emotional abuse, and secretive behaviors designed to keep others from finding out. The simple fact that you *want* to keep things secret is a huge *danger* sign.

Two choices: If you are in a secret relationship you really only have two choices, make it *not* secret or break it off. Pick your poison; make your decision today.

Two planes

Relationships with members of the opposite gender, or same sex if you're so inclined, grow along two planes—(1) emotional and (2) physical. If the emotional plane moves faster you may become lifelong friends, but you'll always be stuck in the "friend zone." Even if you experiment physically it's highly unlikely to work out and may very well *kill* the *friendship* afterward. At *best* it will be *awkward*. On the other hand, if the physical plane moves faster you'll have a wonderful time but eventually drift apart because you'll find that there's nothing *meaningful* to say to or do with each other outside the bedroom. You probably won't stay friends, but you're also unlikely to become enemies when you break apart. It's only on those *rare* occasions when the emotional and physical aspects of the relationship progress at approximately the *same speed* for *both* parties that you'll set the foundation for a lasting association. That's the basis of marriage material.

Think about it: You can't marry the crazy chick (or dude) who's great in bed, that's a *recipe for disaster*, but if you're both up for a good time you can enjoy it while it lasts. And, you can't marry your best friend if she doesn't find you physically attractive no matter how much you might want to, you simply cannot *force* that to work out. It's no fun thinking about what's *off the table*, but it does provide insight that can help you avoid investing too much *energy* in relationships that are unlikely to last over the long run.

WEALTH

"Without a rich heart, wealth is an ugly beggar."

— Ralph Waldo Emerson (1803 - 1882)

If it's important, sleep on it

Have you ever made a bad decision? Chances are that you have, everybody does, but all decisions are not created equal. Buying the wrong house, for example, can drain your bank account and sap your sanity as maintenance, repairs, neighborhood disputes, and a host of other complications make you regret what you've done every single day. A challenge is that we are often *pushed* into spur-of-the-moment decisions from internal and external forces. We're bombarded with "If I don't do it now, somebody else will get the credit," "I've got to act or I'll lose the opportunity," "I've been searching so long, I don't know if I can take it anymore," and "It's a limited time offer..." Nevertheless, it's vital to look before you leap. If a decision does not need to be made right away, especially if it's an *important* decision like choosing a school, making a major purchase, taking a job, or moving across the country, or breaking off a relationship, take a break and *sleep on it*. Literally. Sleeping lets you simultaneously clear your mind and rest your body. When you wake up, your subconscious will have sifted through the options and you will have a *fresh* set of eyes on the problem, a new perspective. Tired, hungry, worn down, or even just overly excited, and you're bound to make *mistakes*. If there's no hurry for a decision, take your time. The benefit of this simple act is clarity, insight necessary to make the best decision that you're capable of.

Action tip: To gain additional benefit from sleeping on problems, take a piece of paper, draw a line down the middle, and list the *pros* on one side of the page and the *cons* on the other. You don't need an exhaustive list, but do try to hit the main points and be reasonably holistic. Don't do this on a computer, however, there's a mind-body connection that comes from handwriting that you won't often find with other media. Making this list gets you thinking, and it helps your subconscious continue the evaluation process while you sleep.

Banks are not your friend

Banks are in the business of making money. For them to earn a profit, they must separate you from your hard-earned money. Now, you may know and like people who work at financial institutions. Certainly there are many *good* people who work for banks, but when it comes to handling money they are *employees* first and friends *second*. Despite being staffed by good people, the bank itself is absolutely *not* your friend. Now, here we come to the crux of the matter, the motivational discontinuity... We are not saying that banks are inherently bad, or that making money is wrong, we are simply saying that they should not make their money off you in nefarious ways. For example, there is a trick they pull called "check sequencing." It works this way: Banks take the checks that you have written and cash the largest outstanding check that you wrote first, then the next largest, and so on. The goal of the bank is to deplete your account with the larger checks so that the smaller ones, which you have undoubtedly written more of, are more likely to bounce due to non-sufficient funds if you have miscalculated how much money you have available to spend. A bounced check means that you get charged *higher* fees (and it screws up your credit rating which means even larger fees later on). Is this practice morally right? Well, you must honor your commitments, not write bad checks, but the bank is playing a game of "gotcha" by *rigging the system in their favor*. They do the same thing with interest rates on credit cards, mortgages, user fees, and a host of other mechanisms through which they earn a profit in legal albeit dubious ways. Indeed, banks may be *necessary*, but they are certainly *not* your friend.

Your smart move: There are banks, and there are *banks*. Community banks, credit unions, and other local institutions who see you as more than a revenue source deserve your business far more than national banks who often do not. If you can join a credit union you'd be well advised to do so. Not only do they limit the games of gotcha, they are also not-for-profit, member-owned institutions who charge *lower fees* and operate with *more ethical* business practices than other companies in their industry. And, they invest in their local communities too.

Zero sum

A zero sum game is based on the concept that if there is a *limit* to something and somebody else has some of it you are unlikely to get as much as you need or desire. It's like fighting over slices of a pizza, there are only so many you can cut from each pie and still feel like you had something to eat. Unfortunately zero sum is also a wonderful way to *manipulate* people to get them to do what you want. Take diamonds by way of example. The value ascribed to diamonds is invented, made up, an affectation of the marketplace. For perspective think back to the Middle Ages when villagers would happily toss the world's largest diamond aside in exchange for an iron ax head or plow shear, something they could actually *use*. Sure, diamonds are pretty, and they've become a traditional way to show how much you love someone, but that's the result of some truly spectacular *marketing*. Jewelry grade diamonds are more aesthetic than practical, and they're *rationed* to assure *scarcity*. De Beers, a company founded over 120 years ago in South Africa, once controlled two-thirds of the worldwide trade in uncut diamonds and still owns mines that produce about half the stones unearthed every year. The company and others like them have stockpiled billions of dollars of diamonds which they carefully release into the marketplace in a controlled flow to assure that there aren't too many for sale at any given time. This practice assures that the stones can maintain their high prices despite the fact that most of the stones dug from the ground today won't be released to the public for *decades* to come.

This is important: Zero sum is a concept, and it's also a mindset. Zero sum thinking means that if you win I lose, so I'm incentivized to do everything I can to keep you down and prevail. The old adage "high water floats all boats" is apropos here. Instead of ordering one pizza and fighting over the scraps, why not order two or three instead? Few things in life are truly win-lose propositions, so zero sum thinking is as *artificial* as inflated diamond prices. Seek to grow the size of the proverbial pie rather than fighting over the number of the slices and you'll be much better off.

ATMs, credit cards, and phone-pay apps

The fastest way to get into debt, and the hardest way to dig yourself back out, is to give in to *impulse buying*. Credit cards, debit cards, and pay-by-phone applications like Apple Pay or Google Pay may be convenient, but they *enable* you to buy anything that sparks your interest without thinking things through, abetting your ability to *squander* money that should have been designated for more important things such as paying the rent, saving for a new vehicle, or becoming the down payment for your future home. Further, there are often bank fees associated with using these payment methods, so you *lose* buying power before you even complete the transaction. These fees can come directly from your bank, the ATM machine from which you withdraw funds or make a cash advance, or from the merchant who charges extra to cover his processing fees. And, *interest* will accrue on any outstanding balances if you accumulate debt over time. In many instances it's better to carry and use cash exclusively, though that's not always possible or prudent (depending on what you need to buy and where you live or travel). If you use credit cards or phone-pay apps, it is imperative to guard against impulse buys by carefully budgeting your purchases, reconciling all expenditures, sticking to your plan, and paying off your balances *in full* every month.

Think about it: Do you have the *discipline* to use your hard-earned money wisely? One way to tell is by putting your credit cards in a sealable container, filling it with water, and placing it in the freezer. Then, remove all of the payment apps from your phone (don't just disable, completely uninstall them). Don't touch your cards or reinstall your apps for at least 30 days. At the end of the month, you will undoubtedly find that you have more money.

To consume, or not to consume... that is the question

With all the distractions we face, focus is an enormous issue in today's world. Look at this way, you are told you need to consume, buy, review, and comment about all things at all times. This is the work of *marketers*, the very same folks who have you gladly paying $5.00 for what used to be a 50-cent cup of coffee so that you can feel the Starbucks *experience*. Their job is to create a need, or maybe a desire, and make it clear to you that without the product or service or information that they're hawking you're somehow *less* of a man, a suboptimal human being. No, this is not illegal, or even morally wrong truly, but it does become problematic when you are not a good gatekeeper of your *mind* and of your *time*. It is up to you to tune out the ad, turn off the smartphone, shut down the social media app, or simply walk away and do something more *valuable*. The more you consume, the more you become cluttered, ad-confused so to speak.

The difference maker: We all have a limited lifespan, a set allotment of hours in our day, and a limited amount of earning potential throughout our lifetime. That we cannot change, but we can decide how *effectively* we will utilize that schedule and resources. While it's fine to kick back and lose ourselves in a movie or television show, become absorbed with social media, or even splurge on something frivolous from time to time, there are far more valuable endeavors that we can pursue other than these things. If you want to retire rich, *budget your money*. If you want to die enriched, *budget your time*.

Saving yourself with savings

It's hard to think about the future when you're young, and you don't always need to, but when it comes to living a meaningful life it's imperative to start planning as early as possible. You need to start *saving*. It's just that simple, start saving *right now*. Here's why: Money is representation of your life's energy, an exchange for your time, skill, and experience for something that you can use to purchase the things you need and desire. Money is valuable, but seriously, what in life is more *precious* than your time? Once it is passed, it's *gone*, never to be revisited. If you don't put away a substantial nest egg when you're young you may have to work your whole life without ever retiring, without the opportunity to *enjoy* the leisure that should come from your toil. That is why you must save for your future and start doing it now. It's a simple equation: Save early, live well.

Give this a whirl: Albert Einstein (1879 – 1955) reportedly quipped that that compound interest is, "The greatest invention in human history." You can think of it as interest on interest, and will make your savings grow far *faster* than you might think. For example, if you invest just $1,000 today and then add a mere $100 a month into your account for ten years at 10% interest, it will grow into $21,718.65. After twenty years it will be worth $75,457.50. In forty it will grow to $576,370.32, and after fifty years your investment will be worth a whopping $1,514,081.09. The earlier you start, and the longer you save, the better off you will be. Don't put it off another day.

The Stanford marshmallow experiment

In the late 1960's Stanford University psychology professor Walter Mischel (1930 -) performed a famous study that became known as the "Stanford marshmallow experiment." The experiment worked this way: They took a group of little kids and showed them a small treat such as a marshmallow or a cookie. The person offering the treat, the tester, told the study group that he or she was going to leave the room and offered each kid a choice. If the child did not eat the marshmallow right away while the tester was gone, he or she could have two treats when the tester came back into the room. Some kids took the small treat for instant gratification while others patiently *waited* for as long as 20 minutes to get the larger one. When the psychologists followed up years after the experiment was first conducted, they discovered that those subjects who had *waited* for the larger reward experienced *more* fulfilling lives, earned *higher* test scores, and were *less* prone to obesity than those who did not, proving the power of *self-discipline*. Let's face it, what was true back then is still true today. Real men can *defer* gratification for the hope of larger reward, whereas boys who cannot see into the future have difficulty doing the right things.

You're not a child: Learn to delay gratification by focusing on the larger things in life, the important stuff that's worth waiting for. Impulse buys, binge eating, drinking, or drugging, and road rage are all examples *childish* behaviors that you should have outgrown as a teenager. Self-control is a vital part of adulthood.

The road to hell is paved with student loans

College isn't for everyone, and there's nothing wrong with trade skills or other alternatives, but an awful lot of high school graduates opt to immediately go for a more advanced degree because of the *opportunities* that a college education brings. Nevertheless, if you can swing college *without* a student loan, you would be well advised to do it. There are good aspects to student loans, they make otherwise unaffordable things doable, but there are *significant* downsides as well. Here is what they tell you, but you don't always hear: Your student loan is *due* six months after you leave college, with a degree or without one. You *must* repay the loan, and if you don't make all the required payments on time they will garnish your wages (which means that your employer is forced by law to take the money you owe out of your paycheck before you receive it). Worse yet, in most cases student loans are non-dischargeable, which means that you're *never* off the hook, even if you declare bankruptcy. If, for example, you are in a horrific car accident that leaves you a quadriplegic who is never able to work again, you still have that loan hanging over your head like the Sword of Damocles. In fact, unless you are able to negotiate a waiver with the government, you will still owe the debt *no matter what*. Even if you *die* the loan is not necessarily forgiven! If your parents co-signed as guarantors, now *they* owe the money, and if they cannot pay their assets will be seized. If you're married (even a common law marriage, which means living together for a certain length of time) they can go after your spouse in most jurisdictions too. So, take out a loan if you really, truly need it, but keep it as *small* as possible. And, know what you have obligated yourself (and your loved ones) to financially.

Listen up: Average student loan debt in the United States has been growing for decades. It reached $30,867 in 2015 and is expected to continue to climb far into the foreseeable future. In fact, 71% of bachelor's degree recipients will graduate with a loan compared with less than half twenty years ago. Some graduates leave college with well over $200,000 in debt, only to discover they cannot find a job that pays more than $40,000 a year *before* taxes and withholdings. That's a really bad equation, one that leaves you under water for a long time to come. Even if it takes you longer to graduate, you are better off working full time and taking classes at night or finding some other *alternative* than student loans.

Pay off your credit cards every month

There's an old song written by Tennessee Ernie Ford (1919 – 1991) about coal mining, called *Sixteen Tons*. Lyrics include the verse, "You load sixteen tons and what do you get, another day older, and deeper in debt. Saint Peter don't you call me 'cause I can't go, I owe my soul to the company store." *Sixteen Tons* is an old country song about a rotten time in history when coal mining companies treated their workers quite *badly*. The workers were stuck living on site next to the mines and could not travel to do basic things like shopping, so the mining companies would sell products they needed at the company store. Sounds like a pretty good arrangement, until you learn that they also charged *premium* prices for the convenience. And, they granted credit to the coal miners who weren't paid enough to make ends meet. Consequently, when payday came around it turned out that many miners *owed the company* rather than the other way around. They quickly found themselves deep in debt, and kept getting deeper and deeper with *no* way of working themselves out. For all intents and purposes they became *slaves* not employees. Credit cards don't work exactly the same way, but they are very similar. You see, credit cards remove barriers to purchase, encouraging folks to rack up *debt*. In fact, scientific studies show that people spend *more* money when they don't actually exchange currency, dollars and cents, and that is just what the company stores wanted in the early days of the Industrial Revolution. It's also what banks and credit card companies *want* today. You spend money with them, more than you can pay at any given time, and carry a balance. Because they make tremendous profits off the interest on those unpaid balances, if you're not careful you will *owe your soul* to their company store.

Simple math: If you charge $500 on your credit card and make only the minimum payments of $20 per month, it would take you 43 months (roughly 3 ½ years) to pay off the balance at 18.9% interest (the average rate most institutions charge). And, it will cost you $686.59. If you continue to use the card and add to that balance every month it could literally take you a lifetime to pay off your debts. If you're going to use a credit card, and most of us need to at some point in our lives, pay off the balance *every* month. If you need a loan, find another alternative. Credit cards are one of the *worst* possible ways you could choose to carry debt because of their high interest rates and fees.

Like death and taxes, it's going to happen

Prices will go up. They always do. It's called inflation. In economic parlance, inflation refers to sustained *increases* in the price of goods and services in an economy over a period of time. For example, the average cost of a new car in 1930 was just $600. By 2013 it had jumped all the way up to $31,352. Over that same period of time average wages in the United States grew from $1,970 per year to $44,321, which means that a full year's wages (ignoring taxes and other withholdings) went from buying three and a third vehicles to just over one, *decreasing* the average person's buying power over time. That same theme plays out for the cost of a new home, a loaf of bread, a gallon of gas, or pretty much anything else you can think of. Sometimes these increases are driven purely by the economic forces of supply and demand, but taxes, terrorism, Federal Reserve monetary policy, war, worry, and other geopolitical forces also play a role. Statistics aside, the important point here is that when *prices rise* your *buying-power falls*. If your salary cannot keep up, you'll dip into savings or investments or go into debt in order to purchase the things you need to *survive*. Consequently you must learn how to hedge against rising prices and protect yourself. You may choose to work with an investment advisor, but don't ever let someone else tell you what to do with your hard-earned money until you are educated enough to *understand* your options and dive in with both eyes open.

Bet on it: As time marches on it's reasonable to expect that greater and greater demands will be placed on your limited resources due to inflation, taxes, and significant life events like buying a home or starting a family. Take a class on investments, such as Khan Academy's "Financial Literacy" or "Finance and Capital Markets" course (both of which are available online for free), and learn about the various investment vehicles you can use to help your savings *grow*.

EDUCATION

"Education is the ability to listen to almost anything without losing your temper or your self-confidence."

— Robert Frost (1874 - 1963)

Setting intent

Whatever you focus on you will get more of. If you put your attention toward getting better grades, then chances are great that you will succeed in raising your GPA. If you focus on making more money, then you will almost certainly make more money. It even works for silly stuff. For example, if you're looking for Volkswagen Beatles or blue minivans, or whatever, you'll almost certainly find what you seek. The rule of focus is just that, a rule, and *it works*. So, if you are focusing on something, especially an emotion, you are going to get *more* of it. For example, if you believe that today is going to stink to high heaven then you will, in fact, discover that it does. Today is national bad driver day, its hemorrhaging rain outside, and they're out of vanilla syrup at your favorite latte stand. On the other hand if you decide that today is going to be awesome, perhaps you will discover that the guy in the yellow SUV let you merge at the last moment so that you didn't miss your exit, the rain has rinsed smog and allergens out of the air so your eyes feel better than they have in weeks, and that barista is kinda cute. When you *set intent*, you virtually always find what you're looking for.

Think about it: Be conscious about *setting intent*. Watch where you put your thoughts as that is the direction you will take. Optimism and pessimism are two views through the *same* lens. Consciously determine which end you're looking through.

Lifelong learning

When you finish your formal education you're not done. The global economy, rapid advancements in technology, and a host of socio-economic and geopolitical factors mean that if you don't keep learning the world will *pass you by*. For instance, when the authors went to school there were no computers in the classroom. Nobody had heard of Bill Gates (Microsoft), Michael Dell (Dell), Mark Zuckerberg (Facebook), or Steve Jobs (Apple) yet. A few decades later and you'd be challenged to find *any* school without computers, or any school kids who don't know how to use them for that matter. This is probably not going to sound good to you because you are likely in or just came out of a school system that is more interested in pushing pupils through classes to earn federal funds than they are to actually helping folks learn, but it's true. Yeah pretty harsh, but truth is truth… Learning all throughout your life is *important*, it creates a vibrancy, makes you interesting, and assures that as the world moves forward you will move forward with it. If you think you are done learning, you have lied to yourself. Every person we know who went to a university, earned a degree, and then went on to work in their chosen field has told us that they learned *more* on the job than they ever did in school. You'll hear the same response from virtually anyone you ask too. These people are successful because they are ready, willing, and receptive to *lifelong learning*. You need to be too.

What it looks like: Lifelong learning takes on all facets of life, not just books or classrooms. Learning through *experience*, acquiring new skills by doing, this has become the greatest avenue of exploration and education for adults. A facet of this you may be familiar with is the summer internship. It helps you take classroom learning, bridge the gap, and *apply* it in real life. If you approach life as a perpetual intern, you'll never stop challenging yourself to learn and grow.

Be a jetfighter pilot

United States Air Force Colonel John Boyd (1927 – 1997) applied the OODA loop to jetfighter combat, and you should apply the same cognitive process to your life too. The OODA loop is this: Observe, Orient, Decide, and Act. This simple protocol can help you make good decisions on a daily basis. It helps you attack life like a jetfighter pilot, aggressively and smartly. Who wouldn't want that? Take a simple task to test this process out, showering. Start by observing the shower, the soap, and towel, orienting yourself, say back towards the water, and then deciding what to wash first and why. Finally you act, carrying out the plan. Now this might sound simple, and perhaps a little silly, but you will likely discover that washing your hair last has you rinsing dirty water over your clean body. How would a doctor who was preparing for surgery go about this same task? A surgeon would have washed his hair first and then moved down his body to assure that he was as clean as possible and didn't re-contaminate anything. Having discovered this fact about the simple task of showering, you have to ask yourself what the OODA loop can do for the truly *important* aspects of your life.

Action tip: Fighter pilots don't burn fuel for fun. Every time that multimillion dollar jet leaves the ground it has a *purpose*. You would do well to adopt such an attitude as well. Think things through and plan them out *before* you act. The OODA loop is a great methodology for doing just that.

Education is a higher power

Nowadays it seems like everyone has a college degree, or aspires to one, but all degrees are not created equal. Science and engineering-related fields tend to bring higher salaries and more *opportunities* than business, education, arts, humanities, and other degrees. And, while advanced degrees can come with more debt, they often bring *more* opportunity than bachelor's degrees. For example, lifetime earnings of employees with master's degrees are roughly $403,000 *more* than for employees who only have a bachelor's degree, and doctorate degrees typically come with a $1,000,000 *advantage* over a person's work tenure than their bachelor's degree-holding coworkers. If you want a higher education there are multiple ways of getting there, but one of the *best* is finding an *employer* who will cover the costs of your advanced degree. Continuing your education while working full time can be a challenge, but one or two classes a semester will advance your career and earning power simultaneously.

Consider this: In many cases if you earn a bachelor's degree and find a job with a Fortune® 500 company (one of the 500 largest in the United States), your employer will *reimburse* you for earning an advanced degree with very few strings attached (such as earning minimum grades and promising to stay at the company for a certain amount of time after graduation). Free or subsidized education is a wonderful kick-starter for your career.

Make it count

While a college degree or specialized training can set you up for success in life, the bare *minimum* necessary to have any realistic chance of a productive future in the United States (and much of the rest of the world) is a high school diploma or General Education Development (GED) certificate. High school is effectively free, paid by tax dollars, yet only 21 states in the US require that students attend high school until they graduate or turn 18. There are a lot of reasons to quit, but even *more* reasons to *stay in school.* Let's start with avoiding jail; dropouts have dramatically *higher* incarceration rates than their peers—about *three* times more than those who have completed their basic education and *six* times more than college graduates. And, they have tremendously *lower* employment prospects and earning potential. This impact varies somewhat along gender, racial, and ethnic lines. For example, Black dropouts are the least likely to be employed (31%) followed by

Asians (43%), Caucasians (46%), and Hispanics (53%). To put it another way, the *unemployment rate* for Black dropouts is a whopping 69%, followed by Asians 57 %, Caucasians 54 %, and Hispanics 47%. And, for those lucky few who do find a job, they earn on average only *one-third* of the salaries made by folks with a bachelor's degree (with a $15 per hour minimum wage, annual earnings before taxes and withholdings are only $31,200 per year). That's a pretty strong argument to *stay in school.*

This is important: Education is an *investment* in your future. No matter how much you hate it, stay in school *at least* until you graduate from high school. And, make sure your friends and family members finish their basic education too. A mind really is a terrible thing to waste.

Learning through adversity

In high school we all run across a teacher or two who just doesn't care, goes through the motions, and does *nothing* to help us learn. As freshmen and sophomores in college we often face "weed-out" classes where a third of the students are expected to *not* pass. Nevertheless just because your teacher is checked out, or acts like a gaping a-hole of epic proportions, doesn't mean that the material he or she teaches isn't *important*. You see, while memorizing the names of dead presidents or the dates of centuries-old battles that took place in foreign lands might not have a ton of utility in the real world beyond academia, virtually everything you learn in class is either a prerequisite for more advanced material or something you will discover a use for at some time in your life later on. Consequently, no matter how little help you receive or how much you struggle it's vital that you persevere and actually *learn* what you're supposed to. Don't just cram for exams and flush the education afterward.

Try this: If you're having trouble with a class *don't* drop out. In some cases you can switch sections to find a teacher you like better, or audit a class taught by another instructor to reinforce the materials. You may be able to find a friend who has taken the class before and done well who can be your mentor. Or, you may have to take an online course that teaches the syllabus in a different way that resonates better for you.

Plays nice with others

In kindergarten one of the nicest complements a student can get from his or her teacher is, "Plays nice with others." That's no reflection of social engineering but rather a nod toward the inescapable fact that if you can't get along with others it's virtually *impossible* to get ahead in life. Group projects in high school and college reflect this same thinking. Even though you're being graded as individuals, the group must be *responsible* and *accountable* to each other or everybody fails. Among other things, this helps you learn how to work in groups, achieve goals, and resolve conflicts, something you can reasonably expect to do every day in the work world. One of the things we discover in group dynamics is that when folks who don't already know each other come together they virtually never mesh right away. Teams tend to go through a phased cycle of figuring out how to work and perform together, something that psychologist

Bruce Tuckman (1938 -) first postulated in 1965 as (1) Forming, (2) Storming, (3) Norming, and (4) Performing. During this cycle the group comes together around a common goal, sorts out who will play what role in achieving it, figures out how they'll realize success, and then begins doing the work. Many folks add a fifth stage, "Mourning," to include the point where a team is disbanded at the end of a project. Understanding and anticipating this team dynamic helps *prepare* you for working with others as quickly and effectively as possible, which is why it's such a big focus in school.

Give this a whirl: There are few skills as valuable for as many aspects of your life as learning how to *resolve* interpersonal conflicts. Sometimes you're a participant, other times an arbitrator, but either way you need to know how to calm things down and work things out successfully. Take a conflict resolution class, read a book, or attend a seminar. You'll be glad you did.

Education is your ticket to the world

Earning a post-high school degree is expensive, time consuming, and difficult, but it's simultaneously your ticket to the world. You see, recent college graduates (between the ages of 25 and 32) earn on average $17,500 per year *more* than their peers who only managed to earn a high school diploma or General Education Development (GED) certificate. Put another way, today's high school graduates only earn about 62 cents for every dollar made by those with a college education. That's one heck of an income gap, and it's projected to *keep growing* wider and wider over time. In fact, most Fortune® 500 companies (the largest in the United States) won't hire anyone who does not have *at least* a bachelor's degree no matter what their skills or experience. In tight labor markets when the vast majority of folks applying for jobs have a degree, it's easy for companies to make higher education an entry requirement. Money isn't everything, of course, but nowadays unless you work in the skilled trades (e.g., electrician, plumber, welder, auto mechanic, or similar) you are likely to find yourself *toiling* for minimum wage and *struggling* to make ends meet without a degree. Sure, there are billionaires who dropped out of college like Mark Zuckerberg, Larry Ellison, and Bill Gates, but they are the *infinitesimal* exception that proves the rule.

Make a note of this: College isn't for everyone, but if you want to provide for yourself or your family don't *settle* for nothing more than a high school degree. Consider trade apprenticeships, community college, vocational school, or military service to acquire knowledge, skills, and experience necessary to set yourself up right.

Learn how you learn

Different people learn in different ways and process information differently, so the better you understand your personal predilections the easier you can acquire and retain new knowledge. In other words, if you know *how* you learn and leverage that information you will be able to grasp what your teachers tell you more *efficiently* and remember it more *easily* than your peers. This is especially important in schools where teachers tend to treat their students like they're all the same despite the fact that research consistently demonstrates that individuals are not only *unique* but also make use of *different* portions of their brains when *learning*. There are seven vectors through which we can acquire information, and everyone makes use of one or more of them during the learning process. These include (1) Visual (using pictures, images, and spatial understanding), (2) Auditory (using sounds, speech, and music), (3) Kinesthetic (using your body and sense of touch), (4) Verbal (using words, both listening and reading), (5) Logical (using math, reasoning, and systems), (6) Interpersonal (learning in groups with other people), and (7) Solitary (working alone and using self-study and exploration).

Your smart move: Everyone uses a mix of learning styles, but most folks find that they have a *dominant* style or two which really works *best* for them. Go online, find a free learning styles inventory, and take the test. The results should prove enlightening.

In college you're the customer

In high school class is mandatory and paid for by other people's taxes, but in college it's an *investment* that *you* have to make. A big one. That means that you're the *customer*, and that you need to *act* like it. For example, sitting through a class where you already know the information is a huge waste of time and money. In many instances you don't have to. If you take advanced placement classes or a "running start" program in high school and test well enough you can earn college credits inexpensively *before* going to university. Once you're there, you can *challenge* many courses by paying a fee and taking a test, writing a paper, or completing a project that demonstrates your mastery of the information without ever setting foot in a classroom. While this is a common enough practice in academia, each college sets its own requirements for what you can and cannot challenge, so you'll need to do a little research to figure out how and when to do it. For the classes you do take, make sure that you actually learn everything you're paying for too.

A good idea: If you feel like a professor hasn't treated you fairly you *may* be able to appeal. Every university has an official procedure for grade disputes, going through the department chair, dean, vice president of academic affairs, office of the provost, or some other official channel. Be sure to bring supporting evidence and communicate *calmly* and *professionally* so that you don't burn any bridges with your appeal.

FAITH

"Hold faithfulness and sincerity as first principles."

— Confucius (551 BC – 479 BC)

The best is yet to come

Simply put, if you believe that the best is yet to come it sets the tone for the hour, the week, the month, the year, even for your whole life. If life in the current moment is hard, it is likely going to get better, especially if you set your mind toward *making* it better. If life is good, then setting your sights on making it even better still is a great *attitude* to have. Sociologically, positive and negative thinking are *contagious*. This happens instinctively, on a subconscious level, which is why folks tend to want to surround themselves with *positive* people. Paradoxically, you can only make yourself more content by thinking happier thoughts when that happy response is at least somewhat believable, so it takes more than hope, it takes *faith*. In this vein, the best is yet to come is an attitude, a shift in intent, and it changes *everything*.

Take one day: Take today and set your intent that today is going to be one of those days where the best is yet to come. Say it and *believe* it. Then, do it again tomorrow. And the next day… Soon you will find that you are looking forward to the next moment, the next adventure to come.

The power of belief

Do you believe in God? Most people do. In fact, roughly 85% of the world's population believes in some type of higher spiritual authority, and many of the rest of us substitute something secular or scientific which we worship with much the same fever. Sociological research demonstrates that religion not only fulfills a powerful human *need* for finding *meaning* in life and death, but also supports the *existence* of society. In fact, most organized religions pull people together through shared stories, rituals, and views of morality. In other words, people who worship in the same way share a joint *culture*, something that's necessary for societies to flourish and grow. Themes like playing fairly, not harming others, being loyal to the group, respecting authority, and living spiritually prevail in virtually all faiths. And, there are two powerful psychological factors that keep these beliefs alive, (1) confirmation bias and (2) disconfirmation bias.

Confirmation bias causes us to pay more attention and assign greater *credibility* to ideas that support our views, whereas disconfirmation bias causes us to expend disproportionate energy trying to *disprove* ideas that we don't agree with. In other words, we cherry pick evidence that supports what we already believe and discount or any ignore evidence that might disprove it. Consequently, if you believe in God or don't, you're *unlikely to change anyone else's mind*. And, the discussion will probably piss them off.

Think about it: Two of the trickiest topics of conversation anyone can have are politics and religion. These subjects touch on deeply held *personal convictions*, where even the most mature and open-minded amongst us are unlikely to change our minds from facts and data alone. As a rule of thumb, *don't* discuss these things at work or amongst casual acquaintances. Save them for your closest circle of friends, and then only bring them up if you're certain you can do so without breaking anyone's feelings.

Being angry at God is part of life

For those who believe, God has a plan for us all. Unfortunately, we have no way of knowing what that plan might be, so oftentimes we don't appreciate it, even rail against it. For example, tragedy or failure may be *necessary*, a growth experience building the strength we'll need for to overcome something even *more* significant farther down the road, yet it could just as easily be *random* fate. We have no way of knowing, and that can piss us off… Truth be told, there is a time when virtually everyone gets angry with God. We are not here to tell you how to handle that. We have been there too, and on several occasions. We are, however, here to tell you that it is *okay* to be angry with God. He can handle it. If you are pissed at God, go ahead be pissed. Deal with what you have to deal with no matter how long it takes or how angry you may be. God's not going anywhere. He is big enough to handle your anger, rage, or hatred, and still look down upon you with love. That pretty much comes with his job description.

Something to ponder: God was here long before you got here and he'll still be here long after you're gone. You cannot understand his plan, no man has that wisdom, and frankly you really don't *need* to. That's what *faith* is for. Relax, you're going to be okay.

The truth about Truth

You *can* handle the truth, but oftentimes you need to play detective to ferret out real data from false and separate fact from fiction. Information and truth are not necessarily the same things, and the basis attached to what we think of as truth often mutates over time. What? Truth is truth you might say. Well, not really... As youths the authors were told that smoking cigarettes was good for digestion, informed by a peer-reviewed, scientific study that pepper causes cancer, and warned that an impending ice age was a clear and imminent threat to all of humanity. Seems laughable now, but let's face it scientists study data attempting to confirm or disprove theory, but theory is *only* hypothesis. Just because one theory *seems* to hold true doesn't necessarily mean that another one is automatically false. Theory is just theory, it's not fact. Heck, doctors "practice" medicine, because they haven't perfected it yet. There's an awful lot that mankind really doesn't know all that much about today... and despite advancements in technology that will almost certainly remain the same tomorrow.

Your smart move: There's a quote from Abraham Lincoln (1809 – 1865) floating around the 'net that states, "Don't believe everything you read on the internet." That's funny because he died a century before the worldwide web was created, but it should also make you think. Don't believe *everything* you read. Check cites and sources. Sometimes what we think of as truth is just a bunch of pundits quoting each other in a festival of hype and hyperbole. Be a skeptic, *do your homework*, search out the facts, and arm yourself with the knowledge to make up *your own* mind.

Wanna dump your religion?

Are you a person of faith? If so, go study your religion. The more you know, the more likely you are to be surprised. You are going to find that, in some instances, your leader didn't say something that you have always taken at face value. We are not saying that some of these parables aren't useful, but we think you will be surprised to find that many of them are not historically accurate. Further, you might discover a wide swath of cruelty and intolerance by so-called "religious" people directed at the weak, infirm, or poor, especially those who held divergent faiths. Historically many religions have done truly ugly things, and frankly as a person of faith you need to be prepared for and able to reconcile that. Our advice, keep things in context, have boundaries, and feel free to call out bad behavior for what it is, bad behavior. Then, be something *better* than what you have discovered. Don't just condemn, but *rise above*. Be more compassionate, be more forgiving, and do your best to understand. Religious history is stacked from floor to ceiling with accounts of brutality performed in the name of God, but cruelty is *not* the exclusive realm of religion by any stretch of the imagination. For example, Chinese communist leader Mao Zedong (1893 – 1976) murdered somewhere between 30 and 40 *million* of his own people through atheistic communist doctrine. So, humans can do bad things. And, frankly, a good way to lose religion is to study religion, but that doesn't have to be a permanent condition.

Look for the boomerang: It is healthy to be repulsed by cruelty. It is also wonderful to seek beauty in all its forms. Keep balance as you learn and know that if you lose your religion during the process, as sometimes happens, you will also need to look for its return. It surely will return eventually.

Dealing with loss and grief

We often associate grief with the death of a loved one, yet virtually *any* major setback in life can cause anguish, things like failing grades, protracted illnesses, financial setbacks, relationship breakups, job loss, divorce, or physical trauma from violence to name a few. In 1969 psychiatrist Elisabeth Kübler-Ross (1926 – 2004) codified five stages of grief based on her studies of terminally ill patients. Any negative change in our lives can bring about those same feelings and we'll find ourselves going through the roller coaster of (1) Denial, (2) Anger, (3) Bargaining, (4) Depression, and finally (5) Acceptance. That's all perfectly *normal*, but sometimes things get even worse and we sink into *depression*. It's important to understand the difference between grief and depression. You see, even in the middle of the grieving we can expect to have small moments of *pleasure*, whereas with clinical depression *emptiness* and *despair* are our *constant* companions. If you have thoughts of suicide, a preoccupation with dying, intense feelings of guilt or worthlessness, or an inability to function at home, work, or school, then it's time to seek professional help.

Reach out: There's a time to man-up and do things all by yourself and a time when it's best *not* to go it alone. If you're dealing with grief it's much easier to get through the process if you *reach out to others* for help. If you don't need a grief counselor or psychologist, you can and should turn to family, friends, a support group, or a spiritual advisor. Regardless of how you do it and what resources you pull in to help, face the feelings and work them through. Unresolved grief can lead to severe depression or worse.

Look to older people for guidance

It is okay, and absolutely vital, that you have a peer group of like-minded people who you hang out with. And it's critical that you have at least a few people in your world who don't agree with you too. This makes for healthy thought, exploration, and fresh intellectual processes. When it comes to the challenges of faith, spirit, and religion, however, there is another group you need to seek out and take counsel from and they are *older* than you. Older people have that essential thing call perspective; it comes from hard-earned life experience. Think of life's journey as climbing a mountain, the higher you go the more you see, the farther your horizon. Older folks are higher up the mountainside, hence have a different, larger view. The longer we have lived the more we experience, and the more we observe through that greater perspective. And, the farther we advance in life's journey, the more we tend to focus on matters of spiritualism as we begin to think more deeply about and come to grips with what comes *next* when our time here is *done*.

When you get a chance: Ask for a viewpoint, not advice but a viewpoint, on a spiritual subject from an older person. We think you will be surprised at the depth of thought and the information you will receive from your inquiry. The value of the conversation is not the answer you receive as much as the simple fact that it will make you *think* a little deeper… and perhaps a little differently.

Loss of faith

Do you feel like you're losing your faith? It is likely going to happen at some point in your lifetime, at least for a while. Sounds harsh, but it's what happens to most of us, so don't get too worked up about it. Relax, this is a time in life of growth and of tests. The simple childish prayers and relationship with God from your youth is *not* likely to survive into adulthood in one piece. It will *transform* into something else. Think of it this way, there is an account from World War II of a Jewish community that, while interned in a Nazi concentration camp, put God on trial. The question they asked was, "Does God exist?" At the end of the trail God *lost*, God *did not exist*. After his decree that God had lost the trial, the community elder paused for a moment and then called for the evening *prayer*. Think about that. Here was a group of demoralized people struggling to survive in a death camp who were praying to a God that just moments before they had, through intellectual argument, *proved* did not exist. These people lost their faith, yet they kept going *anyway*, perhaps praying in hopes that they were wrong. We believe that you too should have this same attitude, this same discipline. It will carry you through those points in your life when you lose your faith too.

Test your faith: Don't be afraid of tests, don't run from the examination, even when it comes to matters of faith. Instead, *embrace* the test and the audits. They will peel away the fat, the childishness, and make what you find in respect to faith stronger and more real.

Acceptance

We come from a very clear position. Both authors believe that there is a God, and that God is good. But, we would *never* push our faith on you… or even on each other. One author is Jewish the other Christian, two traditions that haven't always seen eye-to-eye, yet we get along famously. The reason for this is that we appreciate the journey that the other person is on, the work, the path, the traditions, and know that these are *some* of the factors that make us who we are as individuals. We recommend that you adopt this same policy of *acceptance* and *tolerance*. For example, we both have friends who are atheists, yet we remain friends because none of us mocks or condemns their perspectives. In turn, the atheists respect the fact that each of us has a different tradition, yet common agreement about the existence of a God which they don't believe in. Nobody is hurt, everybody is happy, and we are strong enough in our positions and acceptance that jokes about religion or lack thereof can be tossed back and forth on occasion and no one feels insulted by it. Further no one tries to *convert* any of the others to their *point of view*. Everybody just goes along and gets along. Unfortunately pressuring others into a belief system was not at all unusual; all throughout history, even in modern times, that has been done through harassment, haranguing, or outright violent means. Don't be that guy. Be *tolerant*, respect *diversity*, and know that it is possible for folks who believe in different ideologies to live equally ethical and moral lives.

A little perspective: There's an old saying, "Sweep the sidewalk in front of our own house." It simply means take care of your own business, to make the change where you need to make the change in yourself, and let others do the same thing. We would add that if your neighbor asks for help sweeping his or her metaphorical sidewalk feel free to help out, but don't *force* your way into another person's affairs.

The government wants your faith

If you are a person of deep faith the government will try to kill it, or at least diminish the place that religion holds in your life. If your belief system is strong, however, if it is true, it will survive, but to be perfectly honest the government really does want to become your "everything," to supplant God as the most important aspect of your existence. Self-serving bureaucrats and government officials desire to exert control over of virtually *every* aspect of your daily activities. This might sound crazy, but it's absolutely true, and you can see examples of it in legislation that outlaws plastic grocery bags, specifies what types of light bulbs you can buy, are regulates how much water your flush toilet can use. It's not just a phenomena in the United States, passive secularism, as characterized by official state neutrality toward all faith-based groups and the absence of discrimination on religious beliefs, is now the dominant model in most Western countries. That's all good, yet a collateral impact has been a remorseless push to keep *all* aspects of religion out of public life, such as prohibitions against posting the Ten Commandments on public property on praying on a football field. Government-sponsored secularism tends to lead to political correctness which in turn can push your thoughts toward a place where you don't have to work very hard to kill your faith *all by yourself.*

Know this: When the world tries to root out your belief system, know that it stands ready to replace your faith with a prepackaged system that is ready for you to adopt in its place. Also know that this new system serves *their* purposes, not your own.

GOVERNMENT

"The only maxim of a free government ought to be to trust no man living with power to endanger the public liberty."

— John Adams (1735 – 1826)

The rules are for you, not for them

Alphonse Gabriel "Al" Capone (1899 – 1947) was a famous mobster during the Prohibition Era in Chicago. While booze, bribery, murder, and mayhem made his career, and an FBI taskforce was created *solely* to bring him down, he actually went to jail over *tax evasion*. He spent the first two years of his incarceration in a federal prison in Atlanta, but after he was caught bribing guards he was sent to the notorious island prison Alcatraz in 1934 where his influence was finally diminished along with his ability to reach the outside world. Gangsters like Capone and his modern day counterparts believe themselves *above* the law, or perhaps *beyond* it. Like corrupt politicians they often acquire the money and influence necessary to make that belief a *reality*, but that's not you. You are *not* above the law. In fact you're not only not above the law, you're living squarely *in its crosshairs*. You see, there are goodhearted people in virtually every profession, but there are scumbags and social climbers too. Prosecutors are often ambitious individuals who aspire to higher office. They make the grade, so to speak, through their win/loss record in court and let's face it, you're an easy win. You can be convicted for something as minor as jaywalking, as life-shattering as an underage drinking binge, or as meaningful as murder.

Listen up: You're exactly the kind of person the rules were written for. The nice, generally law abiding individual with *no* political *power* who is easily chewed up and spit out by the system. It may not be right, it may not be fair, but it is the *truth*. Think of this before you act out perniciously.

It's safer to assume failure

You may have heard the phrase, "Hope for the best while planning for the worst." When you are dealing with *any* type of bureaucracy, be it in a government institution, university, or private enterprise, do yourself a favor and assume that they will *fail.* It is the nature of such organizations to have a heavy administrative burden of rules, regulations, paperwork, and more, yet to simultaneously lack *accountability*. This means that the people who work there are more incentivized to follow the rules than they are empowered to serve their constituency. This means that at times the system will fail and also that sometimes the people in charge simply *don't care* that it did. The airline will lose your luggage, the school will misplace your registration, and the cable company will screw up your account, and *you* will be the one who needs to straighten out *their* snafu. This unfairly places the burden of success on you, of course, but don't fret about it. Just assume they are going to fail you and act accordingly to *protect* yourself. For example, when you're trying to solve a problem with a bureaucracy you will need to find the *decision-maker*, not talk to rule-bound flunkies. Create a log, jotting down who you spoke to and what they said along with the date and time you talked as a proof point for any escalations yet to come. With enough determination and perseverance you will *eventually* resolve the problem.

A must: Make copies and keep files. This helps eliminate any single point of failure, assure accountability, and protects you from other people's major malfunctions.

Keep a watchful eye on your government

Every government in every country, from the beginning of time the present day, has done its level best to propagate itself. Those in charge *always* want to take on more power, more control, and more resources. In other words, governments always find reasons to do whatever is in their own best interests, and oftentimes that desire *conflicts* with the best interests of those being governed. For example, President Dwight D. Eisenhower (1890 – 1969), upon exiting the White House at the end of his term in office in 1961 warned the nation against, "The acquisition of unwarranted influence by the military-industrial complex." What Ike (his nickname) was referring to was growth for growth's sake led by special interests, an all too common occurrence to this very day. It is important that you keep an eye on your government at all levels, local, state, and federal, and discern what is real as well as what is not real, and what adds *value* for the constituency. It's not just your tax dollars at risk, it's your *freedom*.

This is important: The government is supposed to work for the people, not the other way around, but it doesn't always happen that way. A root cause of unnecessary growth and wasteful spending is lack of *accountability*. Like a high school popularity contest, voters often choose leaders based on appearance, rhetoric, or unfounded expectations. And they tend to reelect the names they know, even when those leaders are discovered to be narcissistic, incompetent, or corrupt (such as getting caught taking bribes or smoking crack cocaine in a hotel room with a prostitute). Don't be a *lazy* voter. Get informed, get involved, and use your vote *wisely*. It's one of the most important things that free citizens can do.

How society gets what it wants

Laws, rules, and ordinances, these are the way that society gets what is wants. Now understand that the laws are designed to reduce friction, the friction between people. Further, laws are the lowest common denominator, the last definition of human behavior. For example, that's the reason that the cup of coffee you bought from Starbuck's has a warning label on the side informing you that, "The beverage you are about to enjoy is extremely hot." It's because some idiot couldn't figure that out for his or herself and *sued*. Laws are for these people, the stupid ones, the folks who take advantage of others, and the people who *cannot* or *will not* follow the rules that help us live in close proximity yet all find a way to get along. So society, which really means all of us via our elected representatives, passes laws that are designed to keep idiots and malcontents from *harming* everyone else. These regulations give the police their power, granted by us, to make sure your friendly neighborhood sociopath isn't wantonly raping, pillaging, plundering and, otherwise pilfering his weaselly black guts out. That's generally a good thing, but oftentimes we pass so *many* laws that everyday citizens are challenged to move throughout their day without breaking any of them. This means you can get caught up in the system right along with the professional criminals who these laws were meant to address. It pays to have a reasonable understanding of the laws in your local area and how the system works.

Your smart move: Laws, that's how society gets what it wants. Even though you're held accountable you reasonably cannot be expected to know all of them. Nevertheless, you can *learn* about the system and exercise good judgment and common sense. And, you can purchase an insurance policy (such as a personal liability umbrella policy). If you carry a weapon for self-defense or practice a martial art, for instance, you should have a good attorney on retainer in case you have to defend yourself violently and subsequently need him.

You're better than identity politics

All throughout history ruling classes have pursued a variety of strategies designed to keep themselves in power and those they rule in line. For example, French and British colonialists sparked racial, ethnic, and religious tensions in their conquered territories to help assure that the indigenous peoples were too busy fighting amongst themselves to rise up against their occupiers. That didn't always work, as the Revolutionary War in America demonstrated a couple centuries ago, but it's a tried and true formula that's been pursued in many different incarnations since darn near the beginning of time. And, it's still happening *today*. Political consultant Dick Morris (1946 -) said it succinctly when he wrote, "Ever since the days of Roman politics pitting the plebeians against the patricians, the dilemma of the rich has always been how to get the poor to vote for them. They have succeeded in the past by dividing the poor along racial, sectional, and ideological lines." And that's the rub, if you perceive yourself as part of some group, beholden to a certain ideology, it's easy to think of everyone *not* in your group as inferior, to paint them as the bad guys for no better reason than the fact that they believe a few things about which you disagree. Don't fall for that ploy. People are people, we're good and bad, but it's the outcome of our *actions* that makes the determination not the color of our skin, the town we live in, or the politician or political party we vote for.

Action tip: If you consider yourself a conservative, find three things about liberal positions with which you agree. If you lean liberal, on the other hand, look toward conservative philosophy and do the same thing. There are good and bad ideas on all sides of the ideological divide, so don't line up like a lemming and *blindly follow* someone else's lead. Be your own man. Study the issues and make up your *own* mind.

What society wants

Society wants you to play nice with others and pay your taxes. Pretty simple really, the same stuff you learned in kindergarten more-or-less. Problem people cost money and time for society since the government needs to take action to rectify their anti-social behaviors. For example, if someone breaks a law, say committing a strong-arm robbery and assault, society must expend a ton of resources to apprehend the criminal, hold a trial, care for or compensate the victim, incarcerate, feed, clothe, and reeducate the prisoner, etc... It's much cheaper and more effective to *incentivize* folks *not* to cause problems in the first place, so society builds rules that *punish* you for not being a good citizen. No matter how tempting it can be to break the rules or go on an anti-social bent, being a good citizen is not a bad thing. Sure, we romanticize the rebel, especially in Hollywood films, but being an outlaw in real life rarely ends well. It's tough, stressful, and lonely life, and more often than not a short one to boot. Being a stand-up citizen doesn't make you a wimp, Navy SEALs are stand-up citizens and no one would ever accuse *them* of being pussies. Doing what society wants you to do makes you a valuable human being.

The difference maker: You can live a great life and be a productive citizen by following the laws and doing your best to get along with your fellow man. When others follow the established regulations too, things go smoothly just like driving on the highway where everyone *understands* the rules of the road and *follows* expectations. It's the distracted driver, the drunk, the guy who goes the wrong way up the off-ramp who is a danger to himself and others. Don't be *that* guy.

Pictures of the old Soviet Union

Most everyone you meet will tell you that they want an easy life. They say that with their *actions* if not their words, by doing what's *easy* and taking what's *free*. It is human nature, but it's not all good. In fact it can be quite bad. There used to a time in history, and still is in certain parts of the world, when if you didn't work you didn't eat. An empty belly made men go out and find work, create value, and be creative in doing so. Sometimes that ended well, other times not so much, but the *struggle* made the journey worthwhile. You see, when the focus is *solely* on the basics of existence and nothing more, the people become *nothing more*. Communism was intended to be a system where the basic needs of all citizens would be met, but if you look at the pictures of people from the old Soviet Union you will see a flatness to their faces, a dull glaze in their eyes. There was no spark, no creativity, and no drive toward a higher purpose or something "*more*." There was little opportunity for individuality, no incentive for excellence, so they shuffled around like zombies without thinking or feeling overmuch, and ultimately their utopian system collapsed under its own weight. Today it is possible to get your basic needs met with little effort in America and throughout much of the rest of the world. Folks who get by while living on the dole, or doing the bare minimum, become just like citizens of the old Soviet Union. While their basics needs may be met, they lack the drive, the fire of *self-sufficiency* that changes boys into men.

Ponder this: There may be a *free* lunch, but it's not *costless*. People value what they earn far more than anything they can acquire for free. Earning your way helps turn you into the man you're meant to be. Sponging off others keeps you a child.

Learned weakness

Learned weakness is the act of deferring your safety or responsibility to an authority figure. You have been told you are not equipped to handle the situation yourself and that you need to report it to somebody who will take care of it for you. You are not *allowed*, not old enough, not responsible, or not strong enough to take care of things *on your own*. For example, instead of trying to deal directly with a scuffle on the walk home from school like a mature adult, you are socialized to run and get an authority figure, a teacher, or principal, or police officer. Or let your folks deal with it for you. If you've been offended by a coworker, instead of speaking directly to the person who offended you and working things out like mature adults you are told to walk down the end of the hall and talk to a human resources manager who will intervene. Look, we are not talking about throwing down on somebody here, but in a civil, adult society you need to be able to take care of yourself on solve your own problems. Learned weakness is not normal because it is *learned*. And it's dysfunctional because it's *weak*.

Find the weakness: Take a look at your life and just simply ask the question, "Is there a way that I can take care of the issue at hand without help." In other words, if you can solve it yourself, make like Nike and just do it. That's a far more mature approach than whining to an authority figure to whom you relinquish your power.

The world is full of scandal

In 1850, Nathaniel Hawthorne (1804 – 1864) published a book called *The Scarlett Letter: A Romance*. It is the story is about a woman who conceived a baby due to an adulterous affair and the choices and tribulations that resulted from it. The book is full of twists and turns, and moral and social issues and questions. The title of the book comes from the fact that the woman was required to wear a red letter "A" on her clothing at all times because she was an adulteress. It's an old story and a new one at the same time. Scandal makes for complications. It makes for problems that often affect those around the scandal who had nothing to do with what took place. The world has always been full of *scandal* as Hawthorne's book from over one hundred years ago demonstrates. His book also shows how *messy* gossip-mongering can become. You don't have time for gossip, nor if you have a lick of common sense should you *want* to put your precious resources into the scandal. Run from it.

Your smart move: Even though physical magazine sales have been declining for decades due in large part to the internet, we still find copies of *The National Enquirer*, *People*, *OK!*, and a host of other celebrity gossip rags at the checkout aisle in grocery stores. We also find TMZ Entertainment News online and on TV. Scandals dominate because they drive the news cycle. And, they're a time-suck of epic proportions. Stay away from that nonsense, you have more important things to do with your time.

You get the government that you participate in

People often complain about their government and, for the most part, they have a God-given right to do so… at least until their government says that they do not. Remember, while we may have constitutionally-protected freedom of speech in the United States, many governments across the globe stipulate what members of press can and cannot say. Their citizens have *nothing* resembling freedom of speech. In fact, speaking out of turn often leads to imprisonment, torture, or execution. Further, dissident's family members are made to *suffer* as well. In other words, the penalties for expressing political thought in many countries are deep and cruel, but not here. Today, here and now, we have that *precious right…* and *sacred duty*. We can speak, tweet, and post our minds. We have the freedom to speak, to electioneer, to vote, and with our words and deeds we influence our country and our community. Our participation in the political process determines the government we get. You see, your vote, your contribution, your phone call, your email, they all make a difference in how politicians *act*. When politicians find a parade, a cause they believe their constituency is passionate about, they run to the front of that parade and pretend that they were there all along. That's not leadership, it's parade-chasing, and that's both a challenge and an *opportunity*. You see, by speaking your mind you help *determine* which parades your elected leaders will follow.

The next time: If you want to complain about the government feel free to do so, but don't stop there. Whining is not enough, you must take *action* too. Write an email, send a tweet, place a phone call, join a group, Skype, or send a text. Make your voice heard.

Leadership

"Management is doing things right; leadership is doing the right things."

— Peter Drucker (1909 – 2005)

Learn to tell a good story

Telling a good story is as old as human existence. For centuries there was no written language, oral tradition prevailed. People love stories. In fact, it is shared stories that help create culture and hold society together. Did you know that *The Boy Who Cried Wolf* was written by Aesop (620 BC – 564 BC) over 2,500 years ago? It's ancient in origin, yet remains germane today. Fables and parables endure for this very reason, they are memorable, meaningful, and *relevant*. Stories of adventure, funny happenings, or profound musings, these are some of the best ways to communicate important messages. Learning how to tell a good story, keeping a strong line of thought, a crisp narration, and a focus on the grand culmination of the tale makes for wonderful conversation. People engage with and enjoy you more, and it adds a new level of fun to get-togethers. But, it's not just friendly banter where storytelling is important. Believe it or not, being able to tell a great story is a vital part of virtually every *business* presentation, every new product launch, and every significant staff meeting as well. They need not all be funny, sometimes a sad or wistful story is appropriate, but they do need to be good.

Action tip: Telling a great story is an art, but it's a science too... There are structures and "rules," secrets of tone, intonation, and pacing behind how best to connect with the audience, and they vary by subject matter. While you can search for the fundamentals online, joining a Toastmasters club or taking a storytelling class can be extremely valuable, in part because you will get opportunities to not only learn the whys and wherefores, but also to film and *debrief* your performances as well.

Yes, and …

"Yes, and …" is a phrase that is often used in comedy sketches to forward the moment. The last thing a comedian wants is for their comedic partner to reject what they have just said. Think of it this way, a comedian bursts through the door and screams, "It is raining cats and dogs out there!" If the other comedian replies, "No it's not," that's all she wrote. Boom, end of the scene. No one laughs. The same thing applies to everyday conversations. Try saying, "Yes, and ..." more often. It will put you in the driver's seat, letting you *steer* the course of the discourse. And, people will like you better because you agree with them. It is especially powerful in situations where you are part of group that has been assigned to solve a problem, be it in school, business, or even amongst friends or family members, because it's non-confrontational, keeps the dialogue moving, and helps open others to new possibilities in a meaningful way.

Make a note of it: "Yes, and ..." is more than just a trick, it's a change in mindset that helps you be agreeable while looking for innovative and creative continuances that further the dialogue. While sometimes you really do need to say "no," try to make "yes, and ..." part of your everyday language.

Feed the good, starve the bad

The old story goes this way: A Native American grandfather was talking to his grandson, explaining life. Grandfather said that there are two wolves inside each person. One wolf is good, while the other is evil, and they *always* fight. When his grandson asked which wolf wins the battle, grandfather replied, "The one we feed." Feed the good things that you do, feed the good things that people around you do, and starve the bad. This duality of humanness is expressed across disparate cultures all throughout the world. We see this same concept in the Ying and Yang of the Far East as well as with God and the Devil in Western culture. In virtually every tradition man's noble instinct *battles* against his malicious nature. Day by day, the choices we make determine our *character*, they shape which side wins that fight. If virtually every culture around the world gives you this same warning, the least you can do is listen.

Try this: It's called replacement. Whenever you are tempted to do something that you know is not healthy, don't. If all you do is stop and do nothing, consider that a *victory*. Better yet, stop and do something else, something more constructive. By replacing bad behaviors with better, nobler actions you *win*.

Don't throw your name away

In his play *Othello* William Shakespeare (1564 – 1616) wrote, "Who steals my purse steals trash; 'tis something, nothing; 'twas mine, 'tis his, and has been slave to thousands; but he that filches from me my good name robs me of that which not enriches him, and makes me poor indeed." In modern language what the bard meant was that anything that is stolen from you can be *replaced*, but your reputation, once ruined, is nearly *impossible* to earn back. Whenever we make rash promises we know we cannot keep, whenever we fail to live up to our obligations, whenever we gossip behind our friends backs, take credit not earned, or subvert trust in any way whatsoever we *tarnish* our good name. If you want to earn friends and have the ability to influence other people you must maintain their *trust*, yet it's not just your actions alone that can harm your reputation. Other people can do it too, and not just through identity theft. Be careful about who you keep inside your inner circle as well as who you recommend to others, how you interact online, and what you post, like, or share on social media. For example, if you post or like naked, drunken party pictures on Facebook, current and future employers are bound to learn about it and are not likely to be amused. Guilt by association might not carry a lot of legal weight, but it's a powerful influencer in the court of *public opinion*.

Your smart move: There's a concept called idiosyncratic credit (popularized by Baruch College psychology professor Edwin Hollander in 1958). In essence, it is the process by which we make "deposits" into the emotional "bank accounts" of those who we are close to through good deeds, acts of kindness, keeping our word, and demonstrations of caring. Lying, cheating, stealing, finger-pointing, and other nefarious acts drain whatever goodwill we have built up more quickly than we can ever hope to replace it. Think about ways to maintain a *positive balance* with those you care about.

People will always tear down, build anyway

You need not go any farther than the internet "trolls" and their brutal, self-centered, and cruel social media comments to see the worst in human nature. Part of the reason that keyboard warriors act this way is that they are able to *hide* behind the wall of the web. This is an unshackled example of petty people propped up by the power of *anonymity*. Consider how they write about pop stars, politicians, athletes, and actors, how brutal they can be. "That f&cking moron needs to get his act together," they might pretentiously proclaim. The fact that the athlete or actor they're bagging on has a medical condition, or an alcohol or drug dependency, or is facing some horrific challenge like the death of a child makes no difference to these trolls. They make themselves *feel superior* by pointing to the flaws in the other guy's game. That's not tough love, its hard heartedness.

And, it's dysfunctional in the extreme. Sure, petty people tear others down to make themselves feel good, but you're *better* than that. At least you should be. Don't play that game.

Think about it: There's a world of difference between constructive criticism which helps people grow and condemnation designed to tear them down. People with ill intent tend to make *personal* attacks, speaking in broad, simple declarations such as "He's an idiot," "She's fat," or "What a retard!" Watch for these types of comments from others, but more importantly guard against them *yourself.* If you want to suggest change do it by focusing on *behaviors* or *ideas* rather than on personal *attacks*. That's an approach that is more mature and kindhearted.

Just because

Just because somebody has something that we want does not mean we can't or won't be able to obtain it as well. It simply means they have some *now* and we don't *yet*. Jealously often stems from a false belief that somebody else got lucky, received an unearned windfall, or doesn't deserve their success as much as we do. It's extremely dysfunctional since jealousy's root cause is virtually always within *ourselves* not the other person. In healthy relationships we should always be happy for our loved one's successes (unless they did something nefarious such as sleeping with the boss or stealing from a coworker to get them) and sad for their failures. We prop each other up, not tear each other down. Nevertheless, jealousy is *real* and anyone can succumb to it from time to time. It can ruin our relationships, crush our sense of wellbeing, and left untreated turn us into bitter and resentful people. But, it can be conceivably be a good thing too so long as we use the emotion as a motivator to better *understand* ourselves. When taken as spark for introspection and self-improvement, jealously can be transformed from a *bad* thing into a *good* one.

Hey, listen up: Avoid placing blame on others for your own inadequacies. More often than not when you're feeling jealous how you perceive a situation is completely at odds with how the other person sees it, so the first question you need to ask yourself is whether the emotion is based on *fear* or *anger*. That answer should prove insightful. Armed with this information you can begin to make informed decisions on what, if anything, to do about your feelings. And, it will be easier to let the dysfunctional ones go.

Sports

Both authors have hired employees, and all things equal we'd rather hire someone who played sports at a high level, say college or pro, over someone who did not. Why? Well, because playing sports is much different than watching them. "Yeah, no kidding..." you might say as you roll your eyes and walk away, but hear us out for a moment because this is a real deal. When you play sports you get to peek into another person's *heart* for a moment. You will get to see if your teammate or opponent is *weak*, if they blame others first, or if they are *strong*, smart, or can be counted on in a pinch. This works both ways, other competitors get to see into your heart too. Sports are a place to see and be seen, but the more mature you become the more you will not see the physical acts of sport but rather the hearts of the competitors.

Heart versus body: Desire, drive, duty, competition, and teamwork are just a few advantages that athletes learn that everyday folks may not. Your body and physical skills will diminish with time, but the *will* of your heart endures until its last beat. And, your heart and your character grow together in simpatico.

Being lucky

Are lucky people inherently blessed in some way, or do they make their own luck? In practical reality, being lucky is really nothing more than a state of mind. Being lucky is an expectation, a belief that things are going to break your way. This may seem delusional, but oftentimes it's a belief that can come to fruition because your mindset and attitude enable you to find *opportunities* where others only see *problems*. Here's an example you might be familiar with: Dr. Spencer Silver (1941 -) at 3M was attempting to develop a super-strong adhesive when he accidentally created a low-tack, reusable, pressure-sensitive glue in 1968. He had no use for it until 1974 when a colleague, Art Fry (1931 -), came up with the idea of using the adhesive to bookmark his hymnal and suddenly the Post-It Note was born. This fortuitous accident sells over 50 billion units a year today because the folks at 3M found an innovative *opportunity* for an otherwise *useless*

invention. If you firmly believe that everything is going to be okay, that you're going to get what you need, you open yourself up to possibilities that can make that expectation a *reality*. Now that's not to say that you should foolishly approach life with little preparation or forethought, however. Clearly that's silly. What it means is that if you adopt a positive attitude it can become a self-fulfilling prophecy.

The difference maker: Are you a glass half-empty or a glass half-full kind of person? Pessimism and doubt can hold you back, whereas optimism and open-mindedness will help further your goals. For the next month, make a concerted effort to *find the positive* in everything you see. Then, go back and ask yourself how that perspective has impacted your life.

Try to remove your imperfections

Edward Bulwer-Lytton (1803 – 1873) once wrote, "'Know thyself,' said the old philosopher, 'improve thyself,' sayeth the new. Our great object in time is not to waste our passions and gifts on the things external that we must leave behind, but that we cultivate within us all that we can carry into the eternal progress beyond." That's a truly grand way of saying that no one is perfect, we're all *flawed*, but we're all simultaneously able to *grow* and *mature* every day. It's simply a matter of *wanting* to. Philosophers, motivational speakers, life coaches, and religious leaders, past and present, all say pretty much the same thing in a variety of different ways. Take a deep analysis of yourself, identify your strengths and weaknesses, and then *address* those imperfections that you discover. You have three choices for dealing with your flaws, (1) remove the imperfection altogether, (2) continuously improve upon it, or (3) give up and learn to live with your shortcoming. It takes time and energy to make lasting change, but a decision to take the easy road and *do nothing* is nearly always the *worst* choice that you can make. When you find so many wise people across all times and cultures and perspectives telling you to hunt down your imperfections and change them, you really should listen. No one's perfect, nor can we be, we're human after all, but continuous improvement should be everyone's lifelong *journey*.

Consider this: There's a tool that's often used in business called "Start, Stop, Continue." It's relatively self-explanatory, a structured way of identifying things that an organization or leader should and should not be doing in order to improve. This tool can be applied at the interpersonal level too. Find a close friend, parent, confidant, or counselor and ask them to list the things they believe you should *start* doing, *stop* doing, and *continue* to build upon in order to become a better person. Think long and hard on what they had to say, chose one imperfection to improve upon, and take action to do it. Once you see real progress pick a second flaw to work on, a third, and so on.

Learn to wait well

Learning to wait is an essential aspect of adult behavior. That sometimes means, for instance, that a bad teammate, coworker, or roommate is surely on their way out, and if you just wait patiently the situation will take care of itself. Or, perhaps your significant other's behavior is not what you hoped it would be, but instead of causing a fuss or getting into an argument you can wait it out until they get over that one bad day or realize what they were doing and apologize. This is more than patience, its *prudence*. There are many, many situations where waiting can be your *best* course of action. Waiting is a way to allow things to play out, to run their course in the same way that you would if you had a cold, flu, or low grade fever. There are some things that can be done medically to aid in getting over such illnesses, but the greatest weapon against the common viral infection is very simply to give your body *time*. To wait. There are times when waiting is *not* the right thing to do, such as when somebody is hurting themselves or others, and it takes a bit of wisdom to know when to sit back and when to rush in. Nevertheless, you've likely got a bias for action already so for right now learn how to be patient and wait.

Whoa, that was easy: The next situation that occurs where you think you need to get in the middle, to fix it, try waiting *instead*. Watch and see if it will take care of itself with no effort on your part.

Seek adult behavior

Unless you're the victim of a tragic accident, chances are good that you are going to live more of your life as an adult than you will in any other phase of existence. If you live to be 80 years old, not uncommon these days, and you legally become an adult at the age of 18, you are going to spend three-quarters of your time on earth as an adult. Living those years with childlike behavior is, not a waste exactly, but certainly not the *best* use of this longest phase of your life. That's why you should seek adult behavior, things like accountability, responsibility, reliability, and decorum. You'd better get with the program too, because others are and you will be left in the dust if you don't get on board. Adulthood is a fantastic place to live, but it's not just an age, it's a set of behaviors. Make that your choice.

Try modeling: Find a man who you admire, identify the things that he does (and does not do) that are successful, and do your best to *copy* them. That's what *modeling* is. It has nothing to do with runways and scantily clad women, but rather an attempt to emulate meritorious behaviors you find in others. By imitating role models you can learn how to make their behaviors your own.

WORK

"One machine can do the work of fifty ordinary men. No machine can do the work of one extraordinary man."

— Elbert Hubbard (1856 – 1915)

All ethical work is honorable

Fruit harvester, construction worker, security supervisor, disc jockey, bagboy, fast food worker, payroll delivery driver, salesclerk, U.S. Senate staffer, park maintenance worker, bartender, consultant, tire store employee, martial arts instructor, janitor, and IT manager—these are just *some* of the jobs that the authors have performed throughout their careers. That's a pretty big list, huh? Chances are good that you are going to do just as many if not *more* different jobs. This isn't just about bouncing around until you find the one thing you're passionate about. The days of working thirty years for a single company are largely over, and may well be nonexistent by the time you hit middle age. That means *change*, and a lot of it. The secret is that all ethical work is honorable. However, there is a twist. You must *learn something* from the lousy yet honorable jobs you find yourself doing. If you don't learn you are wasting your time, spinning your wheels. And, you are going to be in the same place a year from now that you are today, perhaps not in the same *job*, but still stuck in the same *place* nonetheless. Engage the honorable work with gusto and integrity... and learn something from doing it.

Stop and think: Where do you envision your next job taking you? What's the next *step* in your *career*? What do you need to do to get there? Importantly, what one thing can you learn at your current job that will help bridge that gap, something you can do now to help set up your future?

You're not done yet

It might look like you have arrived. Maybe you earned a letterman's jacket, or perhaps you were admitted into the National Honor Society, received a promotion at your job, or are on track to be the first person in your family to earn an advanced degree. No matter what success you have achieved, you are not done *yet*. There is always a little more that you can do. To take a simple example: If you finish a test early, you're not done. Go back and check the problems that you have doubts about. No concerns? Go back and randomly readdress a sampling of problems to make sure that you read them all correctly, hence avoided any silly mistakes. This should become your standard operating procedure, your SOP. This means you have to focus on the details of what needs to be done and be certain that it's truly right before you finish. In business we call this *first time quality*, but it's really just the old adage, "Measure twice; cut once." Intuitive, right? If you do the job right the first time you'll have a lot less *grief* later on.

Don't blow it: Being reliable and accountable is a hallmark of adulthood. It's imperative on the job, in the classroom, as part of the team, pretty much in any endeavor. Don't blow it by *cutting corners* or rushing through your tasks. When you think you're done, check again to be *certain*, then call it a day.

Having pride in your accomplishments

You may recognize judo as an Olympic sport, but what you may not know is that one of the tenants of sportsmanship in classical judo is that you cannot tell the loser from the winner by the way they act after the match. Contrast this with practitioners of other sports and you'll see a wide divide. Sure, it's good to take pride in what you have done, but it's *crass* to point, mock, taunt, or put on a public display of your greatness. You don't need an end zone dance, a peacock shout of, "Hey look at me! Look at me!" Little men do these things. Big men know what they have accomplished and don't feel a need to *revel* in it. A nod of the head, a pat on the back, a shake of the hand, or a few words with one's family or friends is sufficient acknowledgement of a job well done.

Go look it up: The top ten greatest NFL running backs do not have a single "signature dance" amongst them. They let their *actions* on the field say everything that needs to be said. And, we respect them more for it.

The people you work with

On average people only work for the same employer for 4.6 years in the United States, and while that duration has popped up a bit recently due to the economy the longer term trend has seen tenure shrinking over time. Consequently most employment is perceived as *temporary*, even when it is full time work. Your coworkers may work alongside you, but they rarely become your friends. When you work with others you are forced to hang out together for several hours a day, but not by *choice*. You may have nothing in common beyond the job. Now you may have a great bunch of people who you work with, and life may seem wonderful amongst them, but when it comes to having some kind of tragedy in your life it is unlikely that you are going to find deep compassion or understanding from your coworkers. Yes, a card, and maybe a sheet cake when you leave the company, but most if not all of them will not be there for the long haul. They'll forget about you a few weeks after you move on. This doesn't make them bad people, it is just they have *their* lives, *their* needs, and other demands on *their* time.

Do this: When you work full time it's easy to get wrapped up in the job and forget about other things, other people. Nevertheless, it is *imperative* to stay in touch with your family. They are in it for the long haul for you, and you should be in it for the long haul for them too.

Do it now!

Do it now! Doing things now rather than procrastinating and putting them off to a later date is the mark of a "can do" personality, a get-it-done man. Reasonably there are certain things, projects, tasks, or conversations which really do *need* to be put off to a later date, a project's flow, a coworker's sensitivity, or more important priorities may take the precedence, but that's not always the case. Many if not most things can be handled with a Do It Now (DIN) attitude. And here is the great secret, when you do something now it doesn't take unneeded space in your head, it doesn't loom, and you are *released* to fully enjoy whatever you are doing in the moments that follow. Living without the weight of unaccomplished imperatives is a *wonderful* sensation. When you get things done now you tend to make more money, build a better reputation, and get ahead in the workplace too. In a world of marginal employees, supervisors love the

DIN guy. He's a fire-and-forget weapon for the boss. DIN reliably gets things done, and gets rewarded for doing them.

DIN: Become the guy known for doing it now. Develop a bias for action. Become the man who can be depended upon for getting it done, and done right, and your career will blossom.

Burn the candle while you're young

One of the richest men in the world, Microsoft founder Bill Gates 1955 -), lived for his job. He built his company by pulling all-nighters, catching a few hours of sleep on his office floor when he was too exhausted to continue, and then diving back into work the next morning. And, he hired people who were much like him. In fact, he once told reporters, "I worked weekends, I didn't really believe in vacations. I knew everybody's license plate so I could look out at the parking lot and see, you know, when people come in. Twenty years ago I would stay in the office for days at a time and not think twice about it. I had energy and naiveté on my side. Now hopefully I am a bit more mellow but with a little extra wisdom." Did you note the terms "energy" and "naiveté" in his comment? Those are characteristics that come with *youthful exuberance*. And, harnessing them while you're young *can* be a great thing. Use that energy early, before your life fills up with other responsibilities such marrying a spouse, starting a family, caring for aging parents, or supporting your community. It's important to have balance in your life, not to live just for your work, but when you're first starting out diving in *wholeheartedly* can be the impetus that *jumpstarts* your career. Part-time jobs aside, the first five or so years of your career will set the trajectory for virtually everything that follows. Advancements, earning power, and opportunities all come from accomplishments which you demonstrate during that time. So, if you're going to burn the candle at both ends, do it while you're young.

A winning program: As time progresses you will need to seek more balance than just work in your life. A good way to do that is to schedule your downtime just like you schedule your workday. Get plenty of exercise, find time to relax, assure a restful night's sleep, and drop superfluous activities that sap your time or energy.

Learn how to say "no"

There's a difference between being nice and being a doormat. The word "no" is powerful. It's a complete sentence, one that should be part of your vocabulary. And, it need not be negative as you might think. You will find in the life that people will accept an *honest* no more readily than they will tolerate poor performance. "Can you help me move on Saturday?" your friend might ask. "No, I'm sorry. Normally I'd be happy to but I made another commitment already." This response is a much better *and* more sincere than saying yes and then showing up late or not at all. The word no is a powerful way to protect your good name, it keeps you from making promises that you cannot keep. It keeps you from overcommitting and doing a half-assed job. Think of is this way, if you say yes and don't show up then you have not delivered on you word. That makes you a *liar*. If you say yes and show-up late or halfway through a project, you are perceived as *lazy*, an underperformer. On the other hand, if you say no and show-up unexpectedly with a can do attitude, you become a rock star.

Never overcommit: When in doubt, use the word "no"… or negotiate the deadline. Either way, make sure that you're pleasant about it. Your word should be your bond. Don't duck responsibility, but don't say yes lightly either.

Focus, grasshopper

Our father's generation was taught that if they wanted to do things well and get a lot done they had to focus on doing only *one* thing at a time. While many Millennials *think* they have moved beyond that sort of thing, that they are really good at multitasking, more often than not they are simply doing a lot of things *inefficiently* more-or-less at the same time. They aren't actually getting more done. In fact, experts estimate that multitasking causes a 40% *loss* in productivity. The ability to focus is an absolute must if you want to be a successful person, but it's actually important just to be the kind of person who others want to be around too. We all know someone who is hyper, flits around, and simply cannot *focus* for any length of time, right? While this could be some sort of untreated medical condition (such as Attention Deficit Hyperactivity Disorder), it's often nothing more than a symptom of *immaturity*. These folks' lack of focus absolutely *dominates* any relationship that they become involved in. They rarely act like they're truly listening or care about what you have to say and every conversation morphs into something about their latest fleeting idea, thought, or desire. We once watched a comedian doing an interview where he was asked, "How do you work-up your routine." He explained that the first thing that he needed was absolute quiet. He went on to say that he got more work done in a shorter period of time working in silence than he ever could if he had to deal with background music or other disruptions. Don't be the distraction in your relationships.

Your smart move: We suggest the Pomodoro Technique to improve your focus. Created by Francesco Cirillo, it's a time management methodology that helps you break work down into short, timed intervals called "pomodoros" that are spaced out by short breaks. This method improves your *concentration*, trains your brain to *focus* for short periods, and helps you stay on top of deadlines. Google it and see if it works for you.

Putting one foot in front of the other

We've all heard the adage, "When the going gets tough, the tough get going," but there's a more important concept at play and that is that you should always put one foot in front of the other. This presents the same message as the fable of the tortoise and the hare. You know the story, the rabbit finally decides that it's time to get serious about the race because he finds himself far behind, yet the tortoise has slowly and continually put one foot in front of the other and crosses the finish line first. Knowing where you're headed is important. The very first thing a person should grasp when starting a journey is that by putting one foot in front of the other and metaphorically stepping towards their goal they will make progress no matter how small of a step they take. Even the *smallest* step moves you *forward*. Another step and you get further ahead than you were the day before. So, that's the message here. Know where you're going and continue to move in that direction no matter how difficult the journey. Eventually you will achieve your goal.

Yeah, I've seen that: Have ever seen the quiet kid in the back of a classroom step forward and accept an achievement award out of the blue with no warning? One foot in front of the other with eyes on the goal, that's how that happened.

Tattoos in the workplace

A couple of decades ago tattoos were rare, something that outcasts like gangbangers, outlaw bikers, and prostitutes might display. Nowadays, they're pretty common. In fact it seems that rebels today are the ones *without* a tattoo rather than those with one. A recent study from the Pew Research Center reported that 40% of people between the ages of 18 and 29 have *at least* one tattoo, and that body piercings are a growing means of *self-expression* in that age group. Individuality is great, but a challenge is that depending on where you want to work your ink may *limit* your career prospects. Over half of your potential employers and hiring managers believe that visible tattoos and piercings are *inappropriate* on the job. Clearly there are more tolerant professions such as software engineering and food services and less tolerant ones like education, law, and financial services, but if you want to keep your broadest possible options open think carefully *before* you place a tat or piercing on any portion of your body that won't be hidden by your work clothes.

A thoughtful approach: Roughly 75% of people get their first tattoo between the ages of 18 and 22, so now's the time to think *carefully* about your approach. Consider the fact that most branches of the military prohibit body art on the face, head, neck, or hands, and forbid sleeve tattoos on the arms or legs. These areas are often seen as unprofessional, hence can be career limiting depending on what you expect to do for a living.

The military—be all you can be… or not

If you think you can *hide* from all your problems by joining the military, think again. Sequestrating yourself from troubles at home by joining up will only cause them to fester and become worse as you have already demonstrated that you cannot face up to your problems first hand. No matter what the situation is—if it's your problem or not—the military will not put up with your BS. They have bigger things to worry about. You are given a number and a job title and an expectation to fill that role; they don't care if you're Mad Max or the pope, you're going to do what is expected to be done. If you *think* that you're the hard man, that the Army, Navy, or Marine Corps cannot break you, *think again*. A military of one kind or another has been around for most of human history and its modus operandi across thousands of years and hundreds of different cultures has *always* been to brainwash and body-wash you until they have *sculpted* you into *exactly what they want you to be*. Therefore, it's *not* for everyone. It is a dangerous environment both in peacetime and wartime. The latter needs no explanation, but you must understand that even in peacetime deaths, dismemberments, and debilitations can and do occur. All that being said, the military *is* absolutely a viable *option* for someone who needs direction, discipline, and education. If you are looking for respect, recognition, honor, lifelong friends, a sense of achievement, a career, excitement, a challenge, and an adventure, then the military *may* be the answer for you, but only *if* you are willing to *work* for it.

Caveat emptor (let the buyer beware): Never forget that the military's primary job is to kill people, break things, and blow sh&t up, so if you put on the uniform you are expected to *go to war* and *fight* if called upon to do so. If you do choose the uniform, wear it with pride. Medals and combat patches are *earned*. Work hard and excel in what you do, but be careful in what you *choose* to do. If you become a combat infantryman or Special Forces operator because it seems sexy, for example, how does that job translate to the civilian world upon retirement?

Every day's a job interview

It was casual Friday, but he was wearing a business suit when he stepped off the elevator. "Hey Carl, you're looking stylish today," I said. "Got an interview?" "Every day's an interview," he replied. I hadn't thought of it that way before, but *he's right*. When you boil it down our jobs are all about solving the unmet needs of the institution we work for. Working *hard* is table stakes, everybody (who isn't on track toward being fired) does that, it's our *results* that *differentiate* us from our peers. That means that we must either increase topline growth or improve productivity, sometimes both, in order to justify our salary and benefits, earn a little job security, and put ourselves in line for pay raises and promotions. And, "invisible" accomplishments don't count. If our bosses don't know what we've done for them they cannot take it into account when evaluating our performance. That means we must let them know. It's not a sales pitch exactly, and it's certainly not self-aggrandizement or baseless bragging, but the more we are able to tactfully move the conversation toward the *value* we provide and the contributions we've made the better off we'll be.

A neat trick: Have you ever heard a politician answer a reporter's question? Rarely do they actually respond to what was *asked*. Instead, they leverage the inquiry as an opportunity to *promote their agenda.* Sometimes it's good to be a politician. Consider your three main contributions, what differentiates you the most in solving your organization's unmet business need, and use them as *talking points* with your bosses like a politician does with his or her stump speech. Just don't be annoying about it.

Finish strong

A couple thousand years ago philosopher Publilius Syrus (85 BC – 43 BC) wrote, "Do not turn back when you are just at the goal." Seems obvious, right, but when a project, a job, an academic semester, or competition is coming to an end, that's when people start to fade. Senioritis anyone? That's not just for school kids… Did you know that more mountain climbing accidents occur on the descent *down* from the mountaintop than on the ascent *up* to the summit? The main reason for this is at that point in the climb the hikers are worn out, mentally and physically tired. Their goal of summiting already being met often means that they have less attentive minds, are still focused on the recent accomplishment rather than the long path that's still before them. Being physically worn out while hiking down a steep incline, not a normal walking angle, also contributes, of course. Like the climber's trek down the mountain, oftentimes when you think something is over it is still incomplete. This is the time to double-down, *refocus* on what needs to be accomplished and how best to undertake it. There is no greater disgrace than having a game in hand and letting it slip away at the buzzer, having a sale that you believed to be in the bag and letting it go to another company at the last moment, or having a great day at work lost due to a lazy, last minute screw-up.

Action tip: Watch for these weak finish phases: "That's good enough," "Let's just get out of here," or the classic, "Good enough for government work." Thinking, saying, or hearing these things should be a warning sign that you are not finishing strong.

RELATIONSHIPS

"Assumptions are the termites of relationships."

— Henry Winkler (1945 -)

Appearance and reality

Knowing the difference between appearance and reality is an absolute necessity in today's world. For example, a fine car, nice clothes, and a friendly smile can hide an evil intent. Serial murderer Ted Bundy (1946 – 1989) was by all accounts a *handsome* and *pleasant* man. He was also a brutal psychopath who started killing in his teens and continued to murder right up until he was incarcerated. One of the most infamous serial killers in U.S. history, Bundy confessed to raping and murdering some *thirty* women before his execution, though he is suspected in many other cases and his total number of victims remains unknown. Those few individuals who found themselves in his sights but managed to escape his grasp did so because they *listened* to their *gut instincts*, saw through his disguise, and didn't fall for what he pretended to be. Appearance and reality can be the same thing, of course, but what really matters most is those *few* instances when it is *not*. Look for the cracks in the way a person may act. You may not be confronted with a serial murderer, but you very well be tangling with an amoral loser who you have no business befriending. Gossiping behind other's backs, breaching confidences, lying, cheating, or being duplicitous, especially in the small things, is a neon warning sign to take seriously.

Look here: If a man will cheat on the small things, he surely will cheat on the big things too. And, you may well be on the losing end. Pay attention to the small stuff, it helps reveal a person's true character. Trust your gut, if you have even an inkling that something is wrong protect yourself by conducting a background check. They're relatively inexpensive yet highly revealing.

Be nice to others

You may have heard that nice guys finish last, that's just silly. Some of the most successful people in the world are nice. For example, billionaires Bill Gates, Warren Buffett, Paul Allen, Richard Branson, Larry Ellison, George Lucas, Elon Musk, David Rockefeller, and Mark Zuckerberg have all pledged to give away at least *half* their wealth to charitable causes. That's awfully nice, don't you think? If they can be nice, *you* can be nice too. Be nice to others. Seriously. Being nice is important, it makes the rough edges of the world a little smoother. There are plenty of jerks out there who get off on causing trouble, but that's not you. Being nice doesn't mean being gullible, however, it simply means being a good person, approaching things with a positive attitude, and not letting the world beat you down. The reason to be nice to others is not because they have earned it, but rather because that's *who you are*... a nice person.

Your smart move: There are few things in life over which you have absolute control and your *attitude* is one of them. People with positive dispositions find opportunities where others only see problems. Oftentimes those around them are willing to make investments on their behalf (such as mentorship, coaching, or sponsorship) that they simply wouldn't do for others who seem less deserving. That's why people who *choose* to be *nice* have an easier time in life than those who *choose* to be *difficult*. Make the wise choice.

Age is a number; maturity is a choice

Truth be told, people who are immature are not popular. They might be for a little while but eventually the class clowns of the world always overstay their welcomes. You will move on to associate with more mature and enjoyable people. That is the nature of man, to associate with folks who believe in accountability and live with all of the rights and responsibilities that come with adult *behavior*. Those who choose, and we really do mean choose, to act in immature ways will find themselves left behind. Do you still associate with 1st graders who aren't younger siblings? You don't. You don't because they are simply not *interesting* to you any longer. They are *immature*. It works that way in all healthy relationships. Where folks find mutual *value* they stay together whereas when they do not they drift apart. That is why high school friends often lose touch if some go to college while others stay behind, even though social media makes it nearly impossible to lose track of those you care about. And, it's why married couples with children often drift apart from their single counterparts. The root cause of these fallouts is not the lifestyle differences, it's the level of *maturity* that comes with different paths and life choices.

Hey, listen up: An ever increasing level of maturity is required as we move through life. That maturity can be the result of circumstances, or a conscious and conscientious *choice*. It's for you to decide, and to live the consequences of your decision.

Toxic people

Radiation surrounds us all the time. It's in the air, the ground, even in our food supply. Fortunately the miniscule amounts that most of us encounter on a daily basis can easily be repaired by our bodies with no adverse effects. However, *excessive* exposure from a radon gas deposit under our home, nuclear weapon, reactor accident, or other radiation source can *kill*. The way to avoid dangerous radioactivity is to limit three things: (1) Time, (2) Distance, and (3) Exposure. Time represents how long have you been exposed to the radiation. Distance is how close (or how far away) you are from the source of the radiation. Exposure describes how much of your body has been in the presence of the radiation in order to absorb it. Now, substitute "radiation" with a person who is causing you pain, and we have a simple formula for how to deal with caustic people. Minimize your time with them, keep your distance, and limit your communication.

You can't escape pain: Just as the sun produces radiation commonly known as sunlight, life produces pain. Neither can be escaped, but they can be *managed*. Limiting time, distance, and exposure to toxic people is sunscreen for your soul.

Don't hang with dogs

There's an old saying, "If you lie down to sleep with dogs you will wake up with fleas." It's trite perhaps, but true as true can be. Hang around dubious characters and even if you don't share their transgressions and you'll be *tainted* by association. You may have run-ins with the police, lose your job, or find yourself under physical assault from things that *other people* have done. So, when you choose your friends stay away from the dogs, the people who rarely think about the future, have few morals, enjoy hooliganism, or live hazardous lifestyles who will try to pull you down into the gutter with them. Hang with a different crowd. A challenge is that if you're already in the wrong group you will need to leave, yet can expect that the ones you've left behind will reach out to you and attempt to pull you back in. You need not be rude, make your choice quietly, and step away. As you do this, the distance you create will help you spot the fleas, the little problems and big hazards associated with these folks and their behaviors, and it will help you keep your distance.

Think about it: Lift yourself up to a higher standard by simply taking one action, choose friends and acquaintances that *lift you up* to a higher level of existence. Stay away from anyone who tries to pull you down.

Earn a reputation for graciousness

Being gracious in defeat is important, yet being gracious in victory is even *more* important. One of the greatest coaches in football history Paul Eugene Brown (1908 – 1991), the man who coached the Ohio State Buckeyes and Cleveland Browns, established the Cincinnati Bengals, and was inducted into the NFL Hall of Fame (in 1967) once said, "When you win, say nothing. When you lose, say less." Mocking, taunting, or verbally abusing those you have defeated be it a team or individual is *immature*—petty, punk behavior. A *real* man is gracious in defeat *and* gracious and victory. Earn a reputation for being gracious, earn a reputation for being nice. And, when your friends decide to be immature, which they almost certainly will do from time to time, avoid jumping on that bandwagon. Take the higher road, go the other way. *Set the example*. Don't be seen by their side acting immaturely. Don't participate in doing the wrong things. This is the mark of a man, and a strong man at that.

Try this: Take a moment before you act and put yourself in the other guy's shoes. How would you feel if you were on the receiving end of your own behavior? Would you see yourself is a man, someone to be respected, or as a child?

Listen for hints

In your peer group, amongst your friends, conversations tend to be casual and can easily become blunt, rude, or even outright cruel, especially when the subject matter includes pointing out flaws or failings within members of the group. In the environment outside your close knit circle, however, people are more likely to beat around the bush, using subtle *hints* rather than directly addressing certain subjects. Important business, social, or personal issues, even ones in *critical* need of repair, are likely to be addressed as hint or as part of an anecdote or story. Seems inefficient, maybe even subversive, but folks who don't know you well cannot be certain of how willing you are to receive or address criticism or constructive feedback. Consequently if they use a hint, story, or deflection, it is a softer way to *demonstrate* an issue that you may *urgently* need to look at. This approach protects the message carrier, *and* it protects *you.*

Unfortunately most guys are *clueless* when it comes to picking up on *subtle* suggestions. That's exactly why these hints should cause you to perk up and pay attention. These hints can be some of the most valuable social direction you'll ever receive as long as you are able to perceive them.

Action tip: Listening takes more than just hearing the words, it requires that you absorb *body language* and search for incongruities, things not said, to determine what the other person is truly communicating. If there is a dichotomy between verbal and non-verbal communication you can bet on the *non-verbal* every time. Do Google searches, find a book, or take a class or two on non-verbal communication. The result will be well worth your time.

Be easy to be around

Have you ever noticed that some folks win friends and influence those around them naturally, whereas others struggle to do the same thing? There's a natural charisma that some are born with and others simple aren't, but in many ways it boils down to *behavior* more than *personality*, looks, or charm. Being pleasant and easy to be around is vitally important to gaining and maintaining *meaningful* relationships. Being short-tempered, rude, or demanding is no formula for success. Oftentimes this concept is a bit harder for folks who grew up without siblings to grasp since they're too used to getting their own way, but humans are *social animals*. Even the most introverted amongst us thrives with solid relationships and withers without them. You will have roommates, coworkers, and other close associations whose goodwill is dependent upon your *temperament*. They may get on your nerves from time to time, but it's vital to remember that you are almost certainly doing the same thing to them. Make an *extra effort* to be nice instead of being short or rude, it will soften the hard edges of getting on each other's nerves and smooth the way for a more pleasant and meaningful association.

The difference maker: People who assume they can do better, be better, and set a good example are easy to be around, whereas those who are self-centered and judgmental tend to drive others away. Seek to improve *yourself* before you even *consider* pointing blame toward others.

The currency of people

The idea of the currency of people is not quite what it sounds like. It is not about the value *of* people, but rather what they value *in themselves*. The currency of people is what motivates them at their core level. Is it money? Could it be prestige? Does status light the person's inner fire? What about friendship? For instance, salary is rarely the sole motivator for taking a job. Folks who choose to work in locations that are convenient to where they want to live have determined that quality of life trumps earning potential. Career decisions can have historical elements that are important too. "My grandfather was the groundskeeper for this minor league baseball team, and so was my father, so that's why I work here too," or "My mom was an engineer and I want to follow in her footsteps." In this fashion other elements of life than money become the currency of the individual. You can look at any part of life in this manner, finding the currency of somebody is a fantastic way to learn how to communicate with them, to enjoy them in a way that you may not have been able to do in the past.

Make a note of it: There's a psychological phenomenon called the "similar to me affect." In essence it means that we tend to *like* and *remember* folks with similar backgrounds or interests, such as those who went to the same school, voted for the same political candidates, or worked in the same occupations. Understanding the currency of people plays into this phenomenon. It helps us understand and connect with others on a *deeper level.* Ask your friends and associates what makes them excited to get up in the morning, what lights their fire. Listen *carefully* and you'll discover what they value most.

Hanging out with the fun crowd

It's easy being the smartest person in the room. It's easy to choose friends who aren't all that swift on the uptake or who act kind of goofy. It's easy, and it's fun, but it is no way to get ahead in life. Surrounding yourself with people who are smarter, better educated, more insightful, or more experienced *forces* you to learn and grow. It's far more enjoyable to be intellectually challenged than to be entertained. Let's make a distinction here: Having a not too bright or even downright dumb but fun friend is fine, but it is not enjoyment. Enjoyment is something much more than *mere* fun. Fun is *short-lived* and easily achieved, whereas enjoyment is *deep* and *earned*. Think of it as the difference between slamming an ice cream cone onto the top of your head for a cheap laugh versus enjoying the taste of the ice cream while holding a meaningful conversation.

Your smart move: Think about your relationships. It's good to have friends, but in many way it's even better to have "honorable enemies," that is a select few folks in your inner circle who confront your way of thinking and *challenge* your assumptions. They knock you off your status quo and force you to *grow*. It takes a high level of emotional maturity and intellectual curiosity to handle this type of relationship but it is almost indescribably valuable too.

Choose your friends; don't let your friends choose you

A "grifter" is a term that describes a person who steals from others using the confidence game. In other words, they gain your confidence, becoming what you think is your friend, and then they set you up in order to take your money. It could be as blatant as *stealing* your identity, your wallet, or your checkbook. Or, it could be something subtler like pumping you for inside information about your work in order to illicitly profit in the stock market, steal intellectual property, or undertake other forms of industrial espionage. Either way, to the grifter you're a *cash machine with legs*, not a human being let alone a true friend. They don't have your best interests at heart. A challenge is that these folks are professional criminals. They earn a living from violating people's trust, tend to be charismatic, and can be very, very good at their jobs. It's hard for decent, well-meaning people to uncover fraudsters simply due to the fact that we don't *think* like the bad guys do. Nevertheless, if you choose your friends rather than allowing other people to choose you, you are far less likely to become the victim of a grifter, con artist, or cheat.

Protect yourself: Meter out trust in small increments. If you discover that you can trust your friends with small things, chances are good that they will prove trustworthy for larger things. On the other hand, if small debts go unpaid, confidences are shared out of turn, or other red flags arise you'll know it's time to cut the other person off, to escape before it's too late.

Two ears and one mouth

The fact that every human has two ears and one mouth makes it pretty clear that nature or God, however you want to measure it, is telling you that you need to listen *twice* as much as you ought to speak. This goes well in social settings, and especially well in business and educational environments. Listen twice as much as you speak and you'll be surprised at how much information you get. It makes life much, much smoother. Leadership guru Stephen R. Covey (1932 - 2012) admonished, "Seek first to understand, then to be understood," and it is fantastic advice. The best way to do that is through *active listening*. Active listening helps with everything from getting along with your girlfriend to dealing with violent criminals. There is no downside to this skill, yet most people do *not* use it, in part because they spend more time thinking about how they will respond than they do paying attention to what the other person is actually saying.

In other words, in most conversations, person A says something and halfway through the sentence person B has decided what is about to be said, has formulated a reply, and is mentally rehearsing his lines. From that point on, person B is not *listening*. Real communication has already stopped. So, listening needs to be *active*, which means paying rapt attention, asking open-ended questions for clarification, and paraphrasing the other person's words to demonstrate and confirm understanding.

The next time: The next time you find yourself in a stressful situation where you want to say something, *don't* do it. Listen twice as much as you speak. What you'll often find is that while you may have a solution in mind, others will step in and solve the problem for you. You not only needn't lift a finger, but they will think you're a great leader for not trying to cram your solution down their throats. At times when you do *need* to intervene, use active listening to ascertain root cause, understand everyone's concerns, and assure that you are doing the right things.

People remember how things end

The "primacy effect" is a psychological phenomenon wherein items discussed near the end of a conversation are easiest to recall. It's sometime called a "last impression bias," and it means that people remember *how things end.* Consequently it's important to make every effort to end on a *good note.* Now that is not always possible because you cannot control all the moving parts of every relationship, but making sure you end with a good comment, a smile, or a kind word can go a long way toward taking base emotions *out* of the game. This can make an enormous difference in how you are *perceived*, even when you disagree with your peers. One of the best compliments you can get, and we know this sounds a little odd, is "I don't agree with him, but I like him on a personal level." This is a statement that is based on how you make others *feel.* It builds idiosyncratic credit and helps those around you focus on the facts or issue that you are trying to convey with less distortion, bias, or irrational disgust. Oftentimes it's even powerful enough to override a disagreement.

It's that simple: Try a smile and a firm handshake at the end of every conversation, whether it was an agreement or disagreement. This simple act can change how the future plays out.

LIFE

"A life spent making mistakes is not only more honorable, but more useful than a life spent doing nothing."

— George Bernard Shaw (1856 – 1950)

Do your best to be a person of principle

It's important not to have floating principles. Values that are plastic, which can be shaped by outside influences or situational ethics, are *not* a good thing. Situational ethics mean that you can easily get caught up in the moment or become *corrupted* by others and unthinkingly do something that you'll live to regret. A strict set of guiding principles, on the other hand, helps you make your *own* way through the world. For example, if you firmly believe that you shouldn't steal, or maybe that you shouldn't cheat or lie or harm others who are not threatening you, then those principles can carry you from situation to situation with certainty. Whether you are experiencing something familiar or unfamiliar, a steady set of values will help you *navigate* through the circumstances. Now this is likely not news, you have almost certainly heard this before, but as you enter college or trade school, join the workforce, and enter into adult life that is the point in life where you will experience a new level of *freedom*, and a new level of *testing*. You become wholly *responsible* for yourself and fully *accountable* for your actions. So the message may be the same, but the test is going to come in ways you have never seen, from odd angles, and packaged in very attractive ways.

Give this a whirl: An easy way to think about principles is to start with the Ten Commandments, even if you're not a religious person, because many of them reflect the norms of Western society. From that baseline scratch out the ones you don't believe in, and add in any others that resonate with you. But, keep the list *small* and *meaningful*. If it's too long it becomes impractical and you won't follow it.

Make your own way

Some people are born with exceptional talent—athletes blessed with abundant strength and fast-twitch muscles, mathletes with eidetic memory, actors with looks and charm—you get the idea, but these things are not necessarily *necessary* for success. Remember the old saw about the tortoise and the hare? Competent, steady progress wins out far more often than not. And, all the natural talent in the world means *nothing* if you don't *use* it. For instance, star athletes often don't know *why* they're on top of their game, it just comes naturally, which is why the best coaches are almost *never* former star athletes. They're the backups, the understudies who had to figure things out the *hard* way, but oftentimes that means that they learn the game *deeper* and more thoroughly than their more athletic peers. Your goal shouldn't be about being the best there is, but rather being the best that *you* can be. It may not make you a world champion, but your best is without doubt an accomplishment worth celebrating.

Action tip: You can't control the genes you inherited (or didn't inherit), but you absolutely *can* control things like your work ethic, attitude, passion, showing up on time, being coachable, doing a little extra, and being prepared. By focusing on these intangibles you may not become the best there ever was, but you absolutely can become the *best* that you are personally *capable* of being.

Know what you're good at

Knowing what you're really good at is important because it allows you to step into the positive. It lets you bring your skills to the forefront for the benefit of yourself and others. Look at it this way, we are often critical of ourselves because we are the person that we know the best. In fact, sometimes we're the *only* one who knows when we've screwed up. We didn't get this right, we didn't get that right, and we hosed-up that other thing… The challenge is that human beings are genetically predisposed to *focus on the negative.* It's an ancient survival instinct, but one that's not much needed in modern times. That's why when it comes to a place where we are really, really good, we need to *pay attention.* That needs to be shared, and shared in a gracious and giving manner. People will respect what you have to offer when you are really good at it and offer to help in a sincere and un-braggadocios way. No one is good at everything let alone great, but there are certain areas where every individual excels. Maybe you're a natural athlete, an intuitive programmer, a big picture thinker, a charismatic leader, or a genius at math. It is important to be good at something, to know what that something is, and then when appropriate to share that goodness with others.

Give this a try: Take a personality test online. Myers-Briggs is a great one, but there are many others that will suit just as well. It can help identify *innate preferences* for things like a tendency to solve problems through either logical reasoning or empathizing, or a need for structure versus a predilection for freestyle thinking. Understanding your brain chemistry in this fashion provides deep insight into your natural *strengths* and *weaknesses*, where you can and will *excel*, how you communicate, what jobs/careers will be easiest for you to embrace, and a host of other important factors that you really ought to know.

Have a master plan

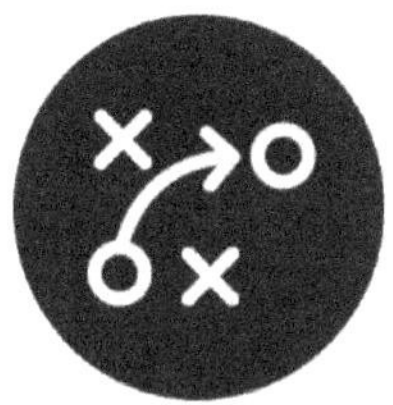

A friend was stuck in a rut. He had no job and no real opportunities. He was living with three other guys and doing yard work and housekeeping to help cover his share of the rent since he had no money to give his roommates. In other words, his life wasn't very together. One day he sat down and contemplated what he needed to do and then wrote out these three simple things on a piece of paper: (1) Get a degree, (2) Get a job, (3) Get a paycheck. This was his strategy, his master plan. Pretty straightforward, and not very deep, but more than enough to get him *off the couch* and back out into the world where he not only earned a diploma but eventually went on to start his own company. The specifics of how he went about doing what he had decided to do, those were the tactics. Get a degree, get a job, and get a paycheck might not seem like much, but it was enough to get *started*. Discovering a penchant for entrepreneurship in business school was enough to *succeed*. Everyone should have a master plan for their life. After all, you only live once so you might as well make something *good* out of it. But, the challenge is that it's really hard to hit something if you don't know what you're aiming for. That's the power of planning. It brings *focus* and *purpose* to your life.

Think about it: Where you see yourself in five years, in ten. What are the three elements of your master plan? Write them down. What are some of the tactics you could employ for getting there? Make a list, and check back in on it from time to time. Those who move purposefully through life tend to be far more successful than those who do not.

Goals and bragging

It's not uncommon to hear people brag about what they're going to do, how big their life is going to be, or what achievements they're intend to make. Further, they often go on to tell you just how they plan to accomplish those dreams too. That's all well and good, truly. A go-getter attitude is *important*; it can carry a person a long way in life. However, if you jump up and down and tell everybody who is willing to listen that you're going to do something audacious such as play in the National Football League and be the MVP of the Super Bowl, well that's an awfully tall order to fill. After all, of the 100,000 or so high school seniors who play football in the US every year, only 310 become college superstars who go on to earn invitations to the NFL scouting combine, and only 215 or so out of that elite group ever earn a roster spot. That's a mere 0.2%! To put it another way, only 1.5% of 5-star high school recruits ever make it to the NFL let alone manage to *start* in a single game. It's good to dream big, but sometimes you're best off having a *quiet* dream so that you do not appear *foolish*. For example, we know of a local kid who played high school football, earned a spot on a college team, and now he plays in the Canadian Football League. He had a goal to *play* football because he loves his game. His goal was simply to play, and then he made the absolute best he could make out of *every* opportunity to do so.

The difference maker: It's good to dream, but silly to get caught up in your own fantasies. In other words, there's a difference between setting high expectations and establishing unreasonable ones. Set *goals*, share your dreams, but be flexible in how you present them both to yourself and others. The best goals are (1) specific, (2) measurable, (3) attainable, (4) relevant, and (5) time-bound, because they simultaneously *challenge* and *inspire*.

Have a plan, but stay flexible

Saying, "I think I'll just go to the local community college" is much different than saying, "I am going to the local community college to study heating, cooling, and air conditioner repair," or "I'm planning to attend the local community college to get my prerequisites out of the way and then transfer to the university." The first statement is no plan, it's just filling time and spending money. The second is a plan, it has a *goal*, a target of where the schooling is going to end. Now that plan might shift around a bit once you've taken a few classes, maybe it takes a little longer than anticipated or the school you choose to attend might shift due to grades and test scores, but there is a plan and it's getting *worked*. Plans that lack direction cannot answer basic questions such as, when you expect to be done, what prerequisites are needed, or how much it will cost to get there. If you can't answer those questions with *specifics* then you have a *dream*. To get out of your dreams and into reality you *must* have a plan, one that has a clear endgame and includes milestones and deliverables for getting there.

Listen to others: When asked about their plans, if your friends use words like, "I'm just," "I'm not sure," or "I think..." they may have an idea but they do *not* have a *real* plan. Are you using these words too? If you are, what does it say about your plans?

Identity foreclosure

Identity foreclosure is something to avoid at all costs. It is a term used in psychology to describe the act of becoming one thing to the exclusion of everything else. We all wear many hats in life, play many different roles. For example, you might simultaneously be a brother, an uncle, a father, a husband, an employee, a neighbor, and much, much more... Nevertheless, identity foreclosure is what *breaks* young and old men alike. The way to see this is by the words that are used. For instance, a high school athlete might say, "I play baseball," or he might say, "I am a baseball player." The first is healthy. What that young man has really told you is that, "I am a person who plays baseball but it's not the totality of my identity." The second statement, on the other hand, *may* be unhealthy. For all intents and purposes he has said, "Baseball is me, and I am baseball." Now that may be just a slip of the tongue, but if baseball truly is life, expressed to the *exclusion* of everything else, other roles and avenues for happiness go away. That is the dysfunction of identity foreclosure. Everybody who engages in it is going to find their world fractured sooner or later, because you *cannot* do one thing for *your whole life.* The downfall can come in many ways, but the results are often tragic and have the earmark statement of, "Oh, man did you hear? [Name] is broke/in rehab/living on the streets." Folks whose profession becomes their whole identity eventually find that they can no longer perform the work, and it's *devastating.* That's why even though very few intercollegiate athletes ever progress into professional sports, student athletes have a harder time than their peers with post-graduation career planning. It's also why people who live for their jobs tend to die within a few short years of retirement.

Your smart move: Listen to the words and the order in which people use them to describe themselves. Is their name first and then their act second, or is it reversed? More importantly, what language do you use to describe who *you* are and what you do?

Flexibility is a great attribute

Being able to see other people's perspectives is a really good thing. To not just reject an idea out of hand because you disagree with whoever said it, but rather be able to entertain the concept, to look at it *objectively* while not necessarily accepting it, and still be able see it for what it might be is a hallmark of *maturity*. In the business world as well as in interpersonal relationships, a strong mind is tested by entertaining other people's ideas whether you like them or not, by accepting challenges to your viewpoint without feeling threatened. Here is an example to try on for size: An Eastern Orthodox monk once said, "Too many choices in the world conspire to take a man's mind away from more important things." In his case, he was speaking of communing with God, of course, but what if you are an atheist? Does the fact that you don't believe in God negate what he said? What if you are Catholic, a Muslim, a Hindu, or a Jew and your religious doctrine disagrees with certain aspects of Eastern Orthodox theology? Whatever you believe spiritually, an overabundance of choices probably *does* make it hard to decide the best thing to do with your time, right? The mature mind seeks the *message* irrespective of the messenger, judges the *content* on its own merits, and makes *informed* decisions.

Pause and think: The next time you are tempted to reject an idea outright, pause. Take a moment later in the day to review your decision. You may still be right, but you may also find nuance and meaning that you had not previously considered.

Strong language, weak language

The Federal Communications Commission (FCC) has banned certain obscene, indecent, or profane language from the radio waves in the United States. Despite the fact that saying things like "sh&t," "f&ck," "c&nt," "c&cksucker," or "motherf&cker" on the air will bring a serious fine and likely cost the radio personality who does it his or her job, dropping an "F-bomb" every two or three words is really not all that offensive to most people anymore. Swearwords are found in popular music, movies, literature, and casual conversations throughout virtually all layers of society. We are certainly not going to tell you that no swearwords have ever left our lips, both authors have resorted to foul language, but we are here to tell you that it is *weak* and *lazy* to do so. Swearing has lost its wow factor, so it really isn't even useful for shock value any more. While some psychological studies have linked swearing with healthy verbal ability, in most instances use of vulgarity simply means that you cannot find the *correct* word or *precise* language to express your thoughts and feelings articulately. And, even if you can, it will often appear to those around you that you cannot.

Hey, listen up: Use your brain, rise above slang and swearwords in conversation, and express yourself in the creative and thoughtful ways that your emotions and views *deserve*. It's more powerful and persuasive than gutter language and makes you appear smarter and more thoughtful too.

Making enemies is no way to go through life

In his fable *The Eagle and the Arrow*, Greek storyteller Aesop (620 BC – 564 BC) wrote, "The shaft of the arrow had been feathered with one of the eagle's own plumes. We often give our enemies the means of our own destruction." Making enemies is *not* a grand idea. Enemies are those we battle against, sparking a war of emotions and resources, yet war should always be the last recourse of civilized societies. War is *expensive*, it places a heavy burden on every aspect of civilization. What's true at the geopolitical level is also true at the interpersonal one. Making individual enemies is much the same as two countries going to war. It's *expensive*, and it costs you in ways that you *cannot predict*. For example, you might think that if that other dude is going to be at the party, it might come to blows, but what you cannot know or anticipate is his level of influence in other aspects of your life.

You need a job with a company where he knows the manager, he makes one well-placed phone call and, poof! No job. Or, perhaps he drops an anonymous tip the IRS and you suddenly find yourself under audit. Or maybe he wages a social media campaign against you, destroying your reputation. It's far *better* and more *mature* to be pleasant, to attempt to make friends with everyone. People generally *want* to be able to say good things about you, so *make it easy* for them. And, at times when you need to walk away, do it in a manner that doesn't create enemies.

Ponder this: The old adage goes, "It is better to be feared than loved." That *can* be true at times, but it takes far more effort to be feared and often leads you to a very bad place in life. It's actually far, far better, and in many ways easier, to be respected or loved.

People will use the system against you

Accusations of racism, sexism, harassment, creating a hostile workplace, and other forms of discrimination are fairly common nowadays. When somebody is unwilling to fess up to a mistake, feels like they have been treated unfairly, wants revenge, or simply thinks they can get away with it, they often point the finger of blame at those around them even at times when they ought to be looking toward themselves first. While the courts are supposed to treat defendants as innocent until proven guilty, our culture—aided and abetted by the 24-hour news cycle and universal social media—has shifted toward forcing many accused individuals to *prove* their *innocence* rather than the other way around, *especially when they're guys.* For example, thirty years ago a fraternity brother joked about handing women he met at college parties a permission form from which they could select a list of sex acts they were willing to perform with him. Back then it was funny. Nowadays it's the law. At least in certain places... In California, for instance, there is an "affirmative consent" requirement necessary to *prove* that intimate contact isn't rape, and that consent can only be given if a person is not incapacitated by drugs or alcohol. Now clearly rape is evil, but the mindset here is that *all* guys are animals and *cannot be trusted.* When your entire gender is perceived as threatening, it puts good guys and bad guys alike at risk.

Be prepared: When you discover yourself in someone else's crosshairs, it's often too late to defend yourself, so it's imperative to act in a manner where you are above reproach as much as possible. Those who know you well and observe how you treat others are more likely to come to your *defense* if you are *falsely* accused of something they would find unbelievable or out of character.

Let's not, and say we did

Boys have poor impulse control. When a parent asks a young boy who is standing over a broken window, vase, or the site of some other mishap, "Why did you do that?" the answer is most likely, "I dunno." Sadly, more often than not that's a *real* answer. No forethought went into the action, boys often make like Nike and just do it. Men, on the other hand, have *impulse control.* Men are able to think about the bigger picture, anticipating any ramifications that may spill out over from their actions. Men *think* first and then *do*. An older friend of ours used to say, "I don't think that is a good idea. Let's not do that, and just say we did." That's good advice.

A better way: Before you do something you may regret take a pause, silently count to three, and then see if it still seems like a good idea. Do it so often that it becomes *internalized*, turns into an automatic behavior. You'll be amazed by how *wise* you become through this simple effort.

Reality break with Marc "Animal" MacYoung

"Spitting blood clears up reality and dream alike."

— Sunao (1887 – 1926)

Let's talk about violence. I have some *really* bad news for you folks. When it comes to violence, you've been *lied to*. And, you've been *set up*.

~~~~~

Violence is, and always has been, a part of the human condition. It's as ingrained a drive in all of us as sex, and about as hard to control. In case you don't know the difference, an *instinct* is a behavior that does not have to be taught (like birds building a nest or flying south for the winter). A *drive*, on the other hand, is something that is very powerful within us, but we have to learn how it works, see
~~~~~

it modeled, and become conditioned in how it's supposed to be carried out in our environment.

So, violence is a drive, not an instinct. That means that *you have to be taught the rules* of how your culture uses it.

The problem is that you've been raised with the *lie* that violence *never* solved anything. That's not only an unsupportable statement, but also an extremist one as well. For that to be true, you'd have to ask every person on the planet, "Did violence ever work for you?" If just one person said "yes" like I would, their response proves that statement is false. Then you'd have to build a time machine, go back, and ask the same question of every person who ever lived.

That's the *lie*. All throughout history violence *has* solved many, many things.

~~~~~

The *set-up* is the fact that you weren't raised with information about how to use violence *correctly*.

Remember, drives have to be taught. In times past you would have learned what was *appropriate*, understood proper levels of force through *social conditioning* and *experience*. For example, when two guys from the same school fought, people wouldn't jump in until it was obvious who had won. Then, they broke it up to assure that no one got seriously hurt. Schoolyard brawls were a big part of establishing social order.

Knowing *when* to stop is another important lesson about violence. Similarly, knowing what behaviors will provoke violence that *won't stop* until one
~~~~~

person is injured or killed is another. Growing up with both of those notions assured that folks knew what behaviors they would *have* to fight for, and what behaviors they would *avoid* if they wanted to stay alive

But, take that socialization away, tell everyone that *all* violence is bad, raise two generations that way, and we find ourselves in a world where *nobody knows what the rules are.*

Zero tolerance policies mean that folks can't *learn* when to stop beating the hell out of someone. Losers don't know how to surrender *safely*, and winners don't know how to *accept* surrender graciously.

Another problem is how many people will get up in your grill using the *threat* of violence and—seriously—believe they're the victim when you smack the hell out of them. This isn't being the *victim* of violence, it's *losing* a fight. But they'll run to the cops and have you arrested anyway.

~~~~~

In today's society someone *has* to go to jail whenever the cops arrive at the scene of a fight. That's usually the winner. So, you may *think* you're defending yourself, but if you go too far—and that very well could mean you look like the winner—guess who is getting arrested and soon be facing at least $20,000 worth of legal costs and fines?

Yeah, *you*.

So, you might want to *pay close attention* to the next few sections.
~~~~~

VIOLENCE

"Men are like steel. When they lose their temper, they lose their worth."

— Chuck Norris (1940 -)

The first rule of self-defense

The first rule of self-defense is "Don't get hit." Ideally we do this by spotting dangerous situations, places, and people, and avoiding them so that we're never in danger in the first place. Professionals call this skill *situational awareness*, which simply means paying attention to your environment so that you know what's going on around you (just like you were taught to do in driving school). In this fashion you can identify and act on factors that are important for your welfare such as looming threats, opportunities, and escape routes. Situational awareness is best used to *not be there* when the other guy *wants to fight*, but it can also be used to *know* when an attempt to talk your way out of a bad situation has *failed*. In this manner you can spot precursors to violence and *avoid* being sucker-punched. Spotting an adversary's "tell" is actually fairly easy once you know the trick, you are simply looking for a *change* in energy, such as when a person who was glaring at you suddenly looks away (checking for witnesses and/or clearing the shoulders and spine to strike), or a person who was looking away abruptly makes eye contact (targeting where to hit). Any sudden change in the other guy's posture, breathing, voice, or skin pallor is a *danger signal*. It may not be an attack, but it absolutely should alert you to pay closer attention and prepare to defend yourself.

Make a note: To practice situational awareness, turn it into a game. Try watching a crowd at a public place such as a shopping mall while pretending that you're a bad guy. Think about who would be an *easy victim*. What is the person doing (or not doing) that makes you think that way? Are they walking upright and paying attention to what is going on around them or hunched over, looking down, listening to music, fiddling with their phone, or staring off into space? Where do their eyes move and what do they focus on? To up the ante a bit, pay attention to who notices you watching them. How do they react?

The second rule self-defense

The second rule of self-defense is "Stop the bad guy from continuing to hit you." Not getting hit is great, but if you've screwed-up your situational awareness and found yourself in a fight you cannot duck, dodge, block, and weave your way out of trouble forever. You'll need to do something more active to *make* the other guy *stop* attacking you. Fortunately most fights end because a combatant feels too much pain and gives up, but a determined attacker may need actually need breaking, something which is very hard to do without using a *tool* such as a gun, knife, or blunt instrument, and such things aren't always available or appropriate (see rule four below). If you need to damage the other guy empty-handed and don't want to hurt yourself in the process, remember the *rule of opposites*—strike hard to soft, or soft to hard. Here's how it works: Try slapping a concrete wall and it might sting a bit, but if you punch it you'll feel real pain. And risk breaking your hand. The same thing applies to punching someone in mouth, you might knock some teeth loose but you'll probably hurt yourself too. This means that you use your hard parts (e.g., knuckles, elbows, knees) to strike the other guy's soft bits (e.g., groin, stomach, solar plexus) and your soft parts (e.g., palm heel, open hand, hammer-fist) to hit his hard areas (e.g., jaw, mouth, forehead). You can apply this rule of opposites to virtually every target on the human body.

Action tip: A Body Opponent Bag (BOB) is a great tool with which to safely practice fighting because it's a relatively soft, human-shaped punching bag that helps you learn how to *contour* while applying the *rule of opposites.* While the rule of opposites is general, contouring identifies the *best target* for any given technique. For example, a single-knuckle strike (hard) fits into the solar plexus (soft) much better than a fore fist punch, even if you only dig your first two knuckles in. Get a BOB, play around a bit, and see what you find.

The third rule of self-defense

The third rule of self-defense is "Always have a plan B." No matter how good a fighter you are, whatever you try is probably *not* going to work exactly like you *expected* it to. You can count on the fact that the other guy will be doing his damnedest to pound your face in, pulling out every trick he can think of in an effort to mess you up. If you try something and it doesn't work that's pretty normal, but if you don't know what to do next you'll likely do the worst thing you can you possibly can—*freeze*. It is imperative, therefore, to have an *alternative* you can move to without missing a beat when things go awry, because sooner or later you know that they will. One of the best ways to do this is by "closing," which means moving to the outside while blocking back across the adversary's body to temporarily tie-up his limbs. This forces him to reposition slightly before he can successfully counterattack, which in turn may give you an opening to move on to another technique, or a moment in which you can safely disengage and run away. You don't have to win the fight necessarily, but it's vital that you *not lose*, so running can be a terrific option *if* you can do it without getting hurt.

Ponder this: The best way to learn to fight is through some sort of martial arts class. Not only do you get competent hands-on instruction, you also get a ton of *practice*. When you're used to solo forms, partner drills, and sparring there will eventually come a time when moving from plans A to B to C is as natural as breathing, even when you're *exhausted* or *adrenalized*. Been there, done that, won't freeze any more. Martial arts aren't for everyone, but if you really want to learn how to defend yourself physically it's your best option. The training can build good character, helping you develop the fortitude to swallow your pride and *not* fight when that's a viable option too.

The fourth rule self-defense

The fourth, and in many ways *most important*, rule of self-defense is "Don't go to jail." You may not realize it, but self-defense is an *affirmative plea* (in the United States). That means that it shifts the burden of proof from the prosecutor to the defense (you). In essence you're telling a judge that you did it—aggravated assault, homicide, or whatever you were charged with—but had really, really *good excuse* hence should not be held responsible for your otherwise *illegal behavior*. You can only succeed with *valid justification* of why you had to do whatever you did, and coaching from a competent attorney to keep you from stepping on any legal landmines. Justification starts with IMOP, which stands for Intent, Means, Opportunity, and Preclusion. To be a *legitimate threat* in the eyes of the law (in most jurisdictions), the other guy must have *intent* (desire), *means* (ability), and *opportunity* (access) to hurt you. If you wind up in court you must be able to show *all* three of these factors in order to justify using countervailing force for self-defense. And, you must be able to explain why what you did was appropriate to the *exact* situation you found yourself in, not simply blather something generic about fearing for your life. Even if intent, means, and opportunity are clear, however, there is one more requirement (for civilians) to satisfy in most instances. You must be able to show that you had *no safe alternatives* other than physical force before engaging. That's the real bugger for claiming self-defense in court, and it is called *preclusion.* If you started the fight or contributed to escalating an altercation to violence in any way you *cannot* legitimately claim self-defense and are likely to be *convicted* of a crime.

Give this a whirl: Go online to a site like Youtube.com and search for videos of real violence, ones that show the events that led up to the physical conflict as well as the fight itself. Thinking about IMOP, who's the good guy, who's the bad guy? Why? Are they both at fault? If you were the prosecutor, what would you say? If you were the defense attorney how would you counter that argument? If you want even more fun, sit in the gallery and watch a criminal trial sometime. It will prove illuminating… and very likely scare the hell out of you.

Know what's worth fighting for

Men commit about 80 percent of violent crimes like homicide, aggravated assault, robbery, and forcible rape in the United States. And, men are also *twice* as likely as women to become victims of those very same crimes, except for rape. So, while bad things can happen to virtually anyone, *men* are the ones who most need to understand *when* and *how* to defend themselves. A significant problem, however, is that younger men rarely anticipate the significant physical, psychological, social, and legal costs that come from violence, so they're often just as willing to fight over stupid things like territory or social status as they are to fight against legitimate threats to their lives and well-being. If you risk spending the rest of your life behind bars, going through painful rehabilitation, being confined to a wheelchair, losing your job, alienating your friends, or declaring bankruptcy as a result of what you do to others or have done to you, is it really worth fighting? In certain circumstances the answer is *yes*, the cost of not fighting is higher than the risk, but oftentimes the correct answer ought to be *no*. The challenge is knowing the difference.

This is important: Every time you fight it has the potential to escalate into something with life-altering *consequences*. Think deeply on that. Ask yourself what's *really* worth fighting for? A whacked-out drug-a-holic lunging at you with a knife in his hands and murder in his eyes, well that's self-evident. You *must* defend yourself, clearly. But, is it worth fighting over a hurtful comment that makes you feel like less of a man? Probably not. What about a carjacker who's trying to steal your fully insured vehicle? Is it better to take the risk and fight, or to hand over your keys and call 911? *Think about it.* Make a list of ten things that you believe are worth fighting for and ten instances where it's smarter to walk away. Check back in a year and see if anything's changed.

Being "hard" makes you unapproachable

You've seen the hard look, right? It comes in many flavors—leather, sunglasses, "tacti-cool" clothing, or buff dude with a thousand-yard stare. That might be great in movies, but not so much in real life. It's simple, if you look hard you become *unapproachable*. Despite the fact that you might think that it makes you look tough, being hard is *not* a good thing. Not only does it cut you off from other people, but it also risks making you a *target* for the *real* hard people, the one-percenters like outlaw bikers, professional breakers, and other hardened criminals. Since fostering a hard look in dress and demeanor is a weak person's *imitation* of power, that's not likely to end well for you. Power fades with time. It's just like the movie starlet who once traded on her youth and beauty only to see it swept away as she aged yet bitterly clings to it, adding make-up, clothing, and plastic surgery in an effort to hang on to the only method that she knows to stay on her game. Men who hang on to "hard" are doing the same sad thing.

Your smart move: There is a world of difference between being *hard* and being *strong*. Seek strength. Strength of character, strength of values, strength of discipline and determination, these things are powerful attributes that do not fade with age.

The escalato follies

"Escalato" refers to the cycle of one-upmanship that takes place during a clash of egos that almost inevitably leads to violence unless somebody breaks off the game. It takes exceptional *maturity* and self-confidence to walk away, however, because all too many people think that it makes them look like less of a man for backing off or giving in. Escalato is an *irrational* commitment because the people involved keep increasing their investment in folly despite overwhelming evidence that it's the wrong thing to do. It's not that the participants don't *know* it's going to lead to a *fight*, but rather that they're playing an *emotional* game of "chicken" to see if the other guy will break off before it gets there. Oftentimes we see this dynamic play out when misunderstanding leads to insult which in turn leads to screaming in the other guy's face, especially in venues where alcohol or drugs or high emotion is involved. If friends don't move in to break things up and give their buddies a face-saving way out, the conflict quickly *escalates* to a shove followed by a flurry of punches, and then things go downhill from there. By the time the dust settles, one or both participants may earn a trip to the local police station, hospital, or morgue.

Pay attention: If you are angry, defensive, or have something you think you need to prove it's easy to get caught up in the escalato follies. The best way to avoid this dynamic is to *respond* rather than to *react*. Responding is a planned course of action, one that leaves you in control of your emotions and actions. Reacting, on the other hand, cedes control to the other guy. Keep your head in the game by remembering that violence is never worth the consequences if all you're doing is trying to prove your point.

Police

Law enforcement officers get a bad rap at times, in large part because more often than not when we encounter them something *bad* is happening. We might be pulled over for a traffic violation, be the victim or instigator of a criminal act, or the cause of a noise complaint. Let's put the police into perspective... Law enforcement officers are *people* just like us, but they are simultaneously *agents of society*. We as a society decide what we think is bad for us as a group. A police officer's job is to stop (arrest) that bad thing if they see it happening, or investigate and bring perpetrators to justice afterward. If you're breaking the law, the police are charged to stop you. Period. End of discussion. That's an officer's *job*. And, since most agencies use dash cams and/or require their officers to wear body cameras nowadays, they cannot be recorded *not* doing their job. Police are not judges, nor are they juries, and while they have some modicum of discretion, don't even try to argue with a police officer—it just annoys them, wastes your time. In fact, if you resist arrest forcefully enough it can get you *hurt* or *killed*. So, be polite and be compliant. Answer questions or don't (as a US citizen you the right to remain silent in situations where you might incriminate yourself), but *always* comply. Do what an officer asks you to do and you won't get hurt. It is a very, very simple formula.

Don't even think about it: Always comply with a police officer's lawful commands. Don't threaten, argue, interfere, or fight. If you are not the bad guy, they will figure it out soon enough. Or a judge or jury will later on... If you disagree with something that happened during your interaction that's what civilian oversight boards, internal affairs investigators, and lawyers are for. Don't try to handle it yourself, especially not during a heated encounter. You *may* be right, but the other guy's got a gun, a badge, and the full weight of society on *his* side.

Learn how to lose a fight

Violence comes in two flavors, *social* and *predatory*. The intent of social violence is to affect your environment (such as trying to impress girls or establish dominance by beating down another guy) whereas with predatory violence it's is either a means to an end (such as stealing your stuff) or the goal itself (such as rape or murder). The easiest way to tell the difference is by the presence or absence of *witnesses*. Social violence *needs an audience* or you can't gain any status by doing it, whereas predators require privacy or stealth to commit their dirty deeds without getting caught and sent to prison. It's imperative to understand these differences because if the other guy is trying to establish status, deliver an educational beat-down, or even gang together with his friends to stake out territory and you handle it right you *might* be able to become friends afterward, or at least not enemies. In a predatory situation not so much... But here's the rub, all too many people nowadays mix the two together, say vengefully returning to the scene of a fistfight with a gun, in large part because their egos are overly invested and they never learned how to *lose* gracefully. A little embarrassment, a black eye, bloody nose, or a few stiches is *never* enough to justify a murder rap.

Stop and think: Martial sports such as taekwondo, wrestling, judo, MMA, or boxing are great ways to learn how to lose—and win—*gracefully*. They build strength, flexibility, fighting skills, and *self-esteem* too. And, win, lose, or draw, they help you gain the intestinal fortitude to get over adolescent testosterone poisoning, swallow your pride, and do the right thing when you encounter real violence on the streets.

A face-saving way out

While professional predatory violence is often devoid of emotion, and something you'll encounter infrequently, *anger* and *fear* are the primary emotional reasons that social conflict escalates to *violence*. If you know what the other guy is angry about you might be able to simply and *sincerely* apologize and walk away without anyone getting hurt. If he's afraid of you, on the other hand, you can simply let him leave, but you need to do it delicately so that he doesn't feel the need to take a swing on the way out to prove his manhood… or come back later with a bunch of friends and a carload of weapons. You see, most of social violence is instigated by young men with *something to prove*, which is why giving the other guy *a face-saving way out* is so important if you want to avoid an *unnecessary* fight. It gives the other guy the opportunity to back down gracefully without needing to strike back to save his dignity and honor. But, it works both ways. Don't get caught up in your own head either. The *tougher*

you truly are the less you should feel the need to *prove* it. If you're secure in your manhood you don't have to have the last word.

Ponder this: Even if you are in the right, it is sometimes prudent to pretend otherwise. Don't let your ego overrule your common sense. Giving your vehicle to a carjacker, your wallet to a robber, or your apology to someone who tries to pick a fight hurts a *lot* less than eating a blade or a bullet.

Dead tigers kill the most hunters

A Chinese proverb states, "Dead tigers kill the most hunters," and it's an excellent warning, particularly when dealing with *predatory* violence. If you find yourself in any physical altercation things can go sideways quickly. You may unexpectedly discover that your adversary has pulled a weapon in the middle of a fistfight, find yourself facing multiple assailants when you thought there was only one, or learn the hard way that the other guy is willing to pull any number of underhanded tricks in order to prevail. A street fight is *nothing* like tournament competition. Bad guys by definition aren't looking for a *fair* fights, they're looking to *win*. There are no weigh-ins, no divisions, no referees, and few rules. And, they rarely choose a victim unless they believe that they have stacked the deck in their favor, setting the time and place for the assault as well as using obfuscation or ambush to conceal their activities until it's too late. Consequently, if you prove tougher than anticipated you can expect the other guy to pull out every dirty trick he can think of to get back on top. Only relax your guard once you have removed yourself from the danger and are certain that you have reached a place of safety.

Important safety tip Egan: Never believe anything an assailant tells you after he throws the first blow. His actions have already demonstrated he's a bad guy. Don't let his words or deeds trick you into relaxing your guard and getting needlessly hurt.

Conclusion

> "Approach each new problem not with a view of finding what you hope will be there, but to get the truth, the realities that must be grappled with." — Bernard M. Baruch (1870 – 1965)

There is a fable about a farmer who had an elderly horse that he used to plow his fields. When the horse got sick, the farmer felt sorry for the poor animal and let it loose to live in the wild for the rest of its short days.

The local people felt bad for the farmer and asked him, "How are you going to work your land without a horse?" The farmer, undaunted, replied, "We'll see."

A few days later the old horse returned healthy and hale along with a bunch of wild horses that followed it back into the farmer's corral. The townspeople joyfully asked the farmer how happy he must be to have so many horses now, yet the even-tempered man replied with a shrug.

The next day the farmer's only son set out to train the wild horses, was thrown, and broke his leg. The people cried out, "How will you work your land with no help?" The farmer, as you'd expect, simply replied, "We'll see."

A few days later war broke out, and the Emperor's men came to town and conscripted all the able-bodied young men to fight, and took all the horses, leaving the farmer's boy behind as he could not go to battle with a broken leg. The story goes on and on... The details are unimportant as you can guess easily enough how it progresses.

~~~~~

The farmer's fable show's that things can be bad, and they can be good, but how you *perceive* them often determines what they will *truly* be. But, there is a bigger issue here. The moral of the story is really about the *core* of the farmer's character. You see, the farmer had a guiding set of principles that carried him through the good times and the bad times alike, a compass that pointed true.

I have flown in private jets, written for world-renown news and information publications, been on national television multiple times, and hung out with rock stars, politicians, and actors. I have also slept on a cockroach-infested floor, rolled in a carpet. At one point in my life I had only 18 cents in my pocket. And, I know that after a little jail time (the case was dismissed) that a meal at Denny's tastes
~~~~~

better than anything I've eaten at Michelin-starred restaurants. Through it all, *I carried my internal compass* and like the farmer's *it pointed true.*

The same scalding water that hard boils an egg turns a potato to mush. It is not the environment that matters, but what you do with it. It is all about how your experiences are measured inside yourself. Do you let them *defeat* you or use them to *learn and grow*?

You too will have ups and downs in your life just like the farmer or me. That is an absolute guarantee. The question isn't about what you'll face but whether or not you can establish an internal compass *to guide you through*, or if you can build a *better* compass than the one you presently have today. Will you meet the challenges, or will you let them crush you?

~~~~~

Do you want to excel in the challenge of life? Do you want to be a man? Do you want to be the best man, the best person you can be, and live a good life through all the ups and downs? Guess what, you're *already* on the right path.

This book has covered a wide array of topics, given you a lot to think about and even more to do, but if you boil it all down to one thing it should be a *commitment* to *do your best*. Do your *best* work in school and on the job, be your *best* self in relationships, and do your *best* to avoid the hazards that the world throws your way. Your best is the least—and the most—you can ask of yourself.

Now that you're armed with the wisdom to make better, more informed choices as you move along
~~~~~

the road of life, put it to use *today* and *every day*. And pay it forward. Be a *role model*, show your friends, family, classmates, significant other, and coworkers what you have come to know. One of the best compliments you'll ever receive is when others recognize your sagacity and begin to emulate what you've done.

So, set the example. Be the best you're capable of, and *show others the way*.

Bibliography

Articles:

- Azar, Beth. "A Reason to Believe." *Journal of the American Psychological Association* (December, 2010).
- Becker-Phelps, Leslie. "The Power of Positive Thinking Put in Perspective." *Psychology Today* (December 7, 2009).
- Bremen, Ellen. "5 Steps to Resolve Your Grade Dispute." *USA Today* (October 23, 2012).
- Brinkley-Badgett, Constance. "How to Qualify for Obama's New Student Loan Forgiveness." *Credit.com* (April 14, 2016).
- Camera, Lauren. "2014 Graduates Had Highest Student Loan Debt Ever," *US News & World Report* (October 27, 2015).
- Couch, Chris. "10 Graduate Degrees with the Most Salary-Boosting Power." *Schools.com* (September 25, 2015).
- Friedman, Jaclyn. "Adults hate 'Yes Means Yes' laws." *The Washington Post* (October 14, 2015).
- Goldberg, Joseph MD. "Coping with Grief." *WebMD.com* (May 31, 2014).
- Goldschein, Eric. "The Incredible Story of How DeBeers Created and Lost The Most Powerful

Monopoly Ever." *Business Insider* (December 19, 2011).

- Hammonds, Keith. "The Strategy of the Fighter Pilot." *Fast Company Magazine* (May 31, 2002).
- Hilton, Andy. "NFL Dreams, Collegiate Reality." *Recruit757.com* (May 4, 2014).
- Holley, Peter. "The Crazy Thing Bill Gates Used to do to Monitor Workplace Productivity." *The Washington Post* (February 3, 2016).
- Kurtzleben, Danielle. "Study: Income Gap Between Young College and High School Grads Widens." *US News & World Report* (February 11, 2014).
- MacMillan, Amanda. "The Multitasking Myth: 12 Surprising Reasons Multitasking Doesn't Work." *Health Magazine* (March 1, 2016).
- Murphy, Geraldine M., Albert J. Petitpas, and Britton W. Brewer. "Identity Foreclosure, Athletic Identity, and Career Maturity in Intercollegiate Athletes." *The Sports Psychologist* (October, 1996).
- Urist, Jacoba. "What the Marshmallow Test Really Teaches About Self-Control." *Atlantic Magazine* (September 24, 2014).
- Wattles, Jackie. "10 More Billionaires Join Buffett-Gates Giving Pledge." *Money Magazine* (Jun 3, 2015).

Books:

- Covey, Stephen R. and David K. Hatch. *Everyday Greatness: Inspiration for a Meaningful Live.*

Nashville, TN: Thomas Nelson, 2006.

- Covey, Stephen R. *The 7 Habits of Highly Effective People: Powerful Lessons in Personal Change*. New York, NY: Simon & Schuster, 1989.
- Greenleaf, Robert K. *The Servant as Leader*. Westfield, IN: The Greenleaf Center for Servant Leadership, 2008.
- Kane, Lawrence A. and Kris Wilder. *The Little Black Book of Violence: What Every Young Man Needs to Know About Fighting*. Wolfeboro, NH: YMAA Publication Center, 2009.
- Kane, Lawrence A. and Kris Wilder. *The Big Bloody Book of Violence: The Smart Person's Guide for Surviving Dangerous Times: What Everyone Must Know About Self-Defense*. Burien, WA: Stickman Publications, Inc., 2015.
- Lombardi, Vince Jr. *The Lombardi Rules: 26 Lessons from Vince Lombardi—The World's Greatest Coach (Mighty Mangers Series)*. New York, NY: McGraw-Hill, 2003.
- MacYoung, Marc. *A Professional's Guide to Ending Violence Quickly*. Boulder, CO: Paladin Enterprises, Inc., 1993.
- MacYoung, Marc. *Fists, Wits, and a Wicked Right: Surviving On the Wild Side of the Street*. Boulder, CO: Paladin Enterprises, Inc., 1991.
- MacYoung, Marc. *In the Name of Self-Defense: What it costs. When it's worth it*. Castle Rock, CO: No Nonsense Self-Defense, 2014.
- MacYoung, Marc. *Violence, Blunders, and Fractured Jaws: Advanced Awareness Techniques and Street*

Etiquette. Boulder, CO: Paladin Enterprises, Inc., 1992.

- Miller, Rory. *Conflict Communication A New Paradigm in Conscious Communication.* Washougal, WA: Wyrd Goat Press, 2014.
- Miller, Rory. *Facing Violence: Preparing for the Unexpected.* Wolfeboro, NH: YMAA Publication Center, 2011.
- Miller, Rory A. *Meditations on Violence: A Comparison of Martial Arts Training and Real World Violence.* Wolfeboro, NH: YMAA Publication Center, 2008.
- Miller, Rory and Lawrence A. Kane. *Scaling Force: Dynamic Decision Making Under Threat of Violence.* Wolfeboro, NH: YMAA Publication Center, 2012.
- Scott, Susan. *Fierce Conversations: Achieving Success at Work and in Life, One Conversation at a Time.* New York, NY: The Berkley Publishing Group, 2002.
- Sum, Andrew, Ishwar Khatiwada, Joseph McLaughliin, and Sheila Palma. *The Consequences of Dropping Out of High School.* Boston, MA: Northeast University Center for Labor Market Studies, 2009.
- Waddington, Tad. *Lasting Contribution: How to Think, Plan, and Act to Accomplish Meaningful Work.* Evanston, IL: Agate Publishing, 2007.
- Wooden, John and Steve Jamison. *Wooden on Leadership: How to Create A Winning Organization.* New York, NY: McGraw-Hill, 2005.

Web Sites:

- Bureau of Labor Statistics (http://www.bls.gov/news.release/tenure.nr0.htm).
- The History Channel (http://www.history.com/this-day-in-history/eisenhower-warns-of-the-military-industrial-complex).
- Interest Calculator (http://www.calculator.net/interest-calculator.html).
- Information on Divorce Rate and Statistics (http://divorcepad.com/rate/).
- Khan Academy (www.khanacademy.org).
- Marc MacYoung's No Nonsense Self-Defense (www.nononsenseselfdefense.com).
- Myers-Briggs Personality Profile (www.16personalities.com/free-personality-test).
- National Institute of Mental Health (http://www.nimh.nih.gov/health/publications/the-teen-brain-still-und`er-construction/index.shtml).
- The People History: (http://www.thepeoplehistory.com/70yearsofpricechange.html).
- The Quotations Page (http://www.quotationspage.com/).
- Toastmasters International (www.toastmasters.org).

About the Authors

Kris Wilder

Kris Wilder is the father of a teenage son and the head instructor and owner of West Seattle Karate Academy. He started practicing the martial arts at the age of fifteen. Over the years he has earned black belt rankings in three styles, *Goju-Ryu* karate (5th *dan*), *taekwondo* (2nd *dan*), and judo (1st *dan*), in which he has competed in senior nationals and international tournaments. He is the bestselling author of over a dozen books including two *USA Book News* Best Books Award finalists and a *ForeWord Magazine* Book of the Year Award finalist. He also stars in two instructional DVDs.

Kris has been blessed with the opportunity to train under skilled instructors, including Olympic athletes, state champions, national champions, and gifted martial artists who take their lineage directly from the founders of their systems. He teaches seminars worldwide, focusing on growing a person's martial technique and their understanding, whatever their art may be. Kris also serves as a National Representative for the University of New Mexico's Institute of Traditional Martial Arts.

Kris spent about 15 years in the political and public affairs arena, working for campaigns from the local to national level. During this consulting career he was periodically on staff for elected officials. His work also involved lobbying and corporate affairs. He was also a member of The Order of St. Francis (OSF), one of many active Apostolic Christian Orders.

Kris lives in Seattle, Washington. You can contact him directly at wskadojo@gmail.com, follow him on Twitter (@kris_wilder), or connect on Facebook (www.facebook.com/kris.wilder).

Lawrence A. Kane

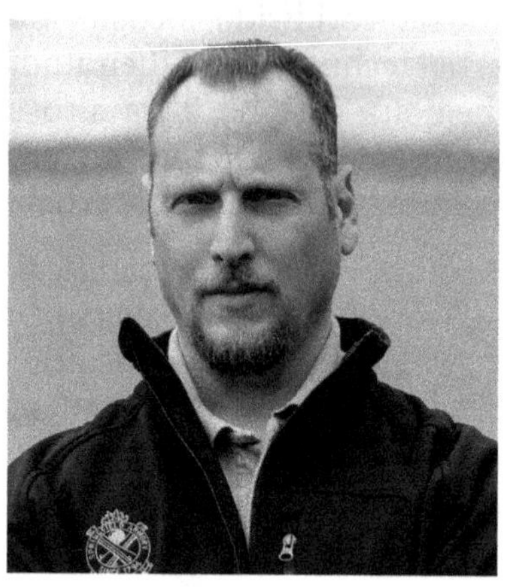

A bestselling author, martial artist, and judicious use-of-force expert, Lawrence's books have earned four *USA Book News* Best Books Award finalists, an *eLit Book Awards* Bronze prize, two *Beverly Hills Book Awards* finalists, two *Next Generation Indie Book Awards* finalists, and two *ForeWord Magazine* Book of the Year Award finalists. A founding technical consultant to University of New Mexico's Institute of Traditional Martial Arts, he also has written numerous articles on martial arts, self-defense, countervailing force, and related topics. He has spoken with journalists numerous times, including once where he was interviewed in English by a reporter from a Swiss newspaper for an article that was published in French, and found that oddly amusing.

Since 1970, he has studied and taught traditional Asian martial arts, medieval European combat, and modern close-quarter weapon techniques. Working stadium security part-time for 26 years he was involved in hundreds of violent altercations, but got paid to watch football. The father of a teenage son, he has seen the trials and tribulations of a young man's life first hand as well as through the lens of a parent, coach, and mentor.

To pay the bills Lawrence works as a senior leader at a Fortune® 50 corporation where, among other things, he is responsible for the strategy for a $1.2B per year organization. He saved the company well over $2.3B by hiring, training, and developing a high-performance team that creates sourcing strategies, improves processes, negotiates contracts, and benchmarks internal and external supplier performance. He regularly advances thought leadership in strategic sourcing, benchmarking, and supplier innovation as a frequent speaker at conferences such as Sourcing Industry Group (SIG) and International Association of Outsourcing Professionals (IAOP). His is also a member of the SIG University Advisory Board, the IAOP Training & Certification Committee, and the Avasant Global Digital Innovation Council (GDIC).

Lawrence lives in Seattle, Washington. You can contact him directly at lakane@ix.netcom.com or connect with him on LinkedIn (www.linkedin.com/in/lawrenceakane).

Marc "Animal" MacYoung

Growing up on gang-infested streets not only gave Marc MacYoung his street name "Animal," but also extensive firsthand experience about what does and does not work for self-defense. Over the years, he has held a number of dangerous occupations including director of a correctional institute, bodyguard, and bouncer. He was first shot at when he was 15 years old and has since survived multiple attempts on his life, including professional contract hits. He has studied a variety of martial arts since childhood, teaching experience-based self-defense to police, military, civilians, and martial artists around the world. His has also written dozens of books and produced numerous DVDs covering all aspects of this field. He codified the five stages of violent crime, is a court recognized expert witness, and developed Conflict Communications, a de-escalation and conflict resolution program with Rory Miller. His websites are www.marcmacyoung.com and www.nononsenseselfdefense.com.

Other Works by the Authors

Non-Fiction Books:

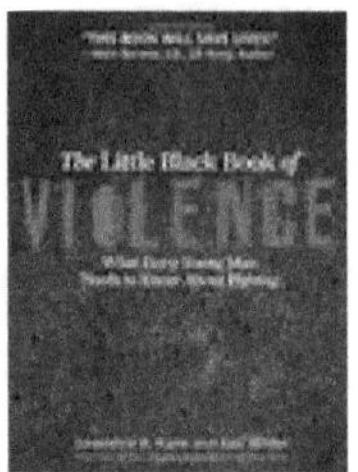

The Little Black Book of Violence (Kane/Wilder)

"This book will save lives!" – **Alain Burrese**, JD, former US Army 2nd Infantry Division Scout Sniper School instructor

Men commit 80 percent of all violent crimes and are twice as likely to become the victims of aggressive behavior. This book is primarily written for men ages 15 to 35, and contains more than mere self-defense techniques. You will learn crucial information about street survival that most martial arts instructors don't even know. Discover how to use awareness, avoidance, and de-escalation to help stave off violence, know when it's prudent to fight, and understand how to do so effectively when fighting is unavoidable.

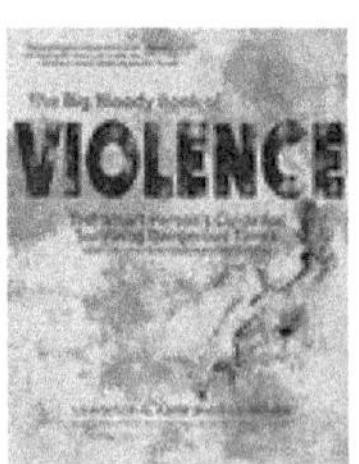

The Big Bloody Book of Violence (Kane/Wilder)

"Implementing even a fraction of this book's suggestions will substantially increase your overall safety." – **Gila Hayes**, Armed Citizens' Legal Defense Network

All throughout history ordinary people have been at risk of violence in one way or another. Abdicating personal responsibility by outsourcing your safety to others might be the easy way out, but it does little to safeguard your welfare. In this book you'll discover what dangers you face and learn proven strategies to thwart them. Self-defense is far more than fighting skills; it's a lifestyle choice, a more enlightened way of looking at and moving through the world. Learn to make sense of "senseless" violence, overcome talisman thinking, escape riots, avert terrorism, circumvent gangs, defend against home invasions, safely interact with law enforcement, and conquer seemingly impossible odds.

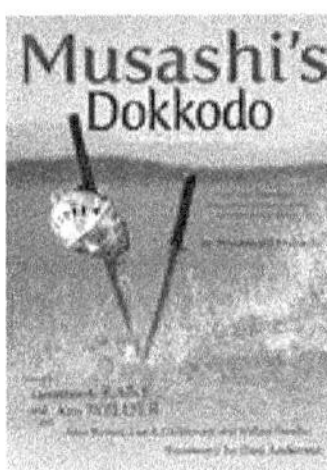

Musashi's Dokkodo (The Way of Walking Alone) (Musashi/Kane/ Wilder/etc.)

"The authors have made classic samurai wisdom accessible to the modern martial artist like never before." – **Goran Powell**, award winning author of *Chojun* and *A Sudden Dawn*

Miyamoto Musashi (1584 – 1645) was arguably the greatest swordsman who ever lived. The iconic sword saint of Japan was clearly a genius, yet he was also a functional psychopath—ruthless, fearless, hyper-focused, and utterly without conscience. Shortly before he died, Musashi wrote down his final thoughts in a treatise called *Dokkodo*. Rather than a simple translation of this important work, this book contains Musashi's original 21 precepts of the *Dokkodo* along with five different interpretations of each passage written from the viewpoints of a monk (Wilder), a warrior (Burrese), a teacher (Smedley), an insurance executive (Christensen), and a businessman (Kane). In them are enduring lessons for how to lead a successful and meaningful life.

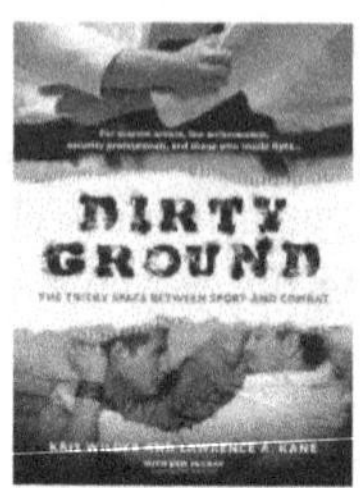

Dirty Ground
(Kane/Wilder)

"Fills a void in martial arts training." – **Loren W. Christensen**, Martial Arts Masters Hall of Fame member

This book addresses a significant gap in most martial arts training, the tricky space that lies between sport and combat applications where you need to control a person without injuring him (or her). Techniques in this region are called "drunkle," named after the drunken uncle disrupting a family gathering. Understanding how to deal with combat, sport, and drunkle situations is vital because appropriate use of force is codified in law and actions that do not accommodate these regulations can have severe repercussions. Martial arts techniques must be adapted to best fit the situation you find yourself in. This book shows you how.

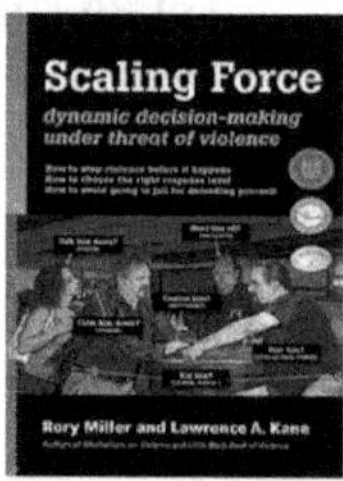

Scaling Force
(Kane/Miller)

"If you're serious about learning how the application of physical force works—before, during and after the fact—I cannot recommend this book highly enough." – **Lt. Jon Lupo**, New York State Police

Conflict and violence cover a broad range of behaviors, from intimidation to murder, and require an equally broad range of responses. A kind word will not resolve all situations, nor will wristlocks, punches, or even a gun. This book introduces the full range of options, from skillfully doing nothing to employing deadly force. You will understand the limits of each type of force, when specific levels may be appropriate, the circumstances under which you may have to apply them, and the potential costs, legally and personally, of your decision. If you do not know how to succeed at all six levels covered in this book there are situations in which you will have no appropriate options. More often than not, that will end badly.

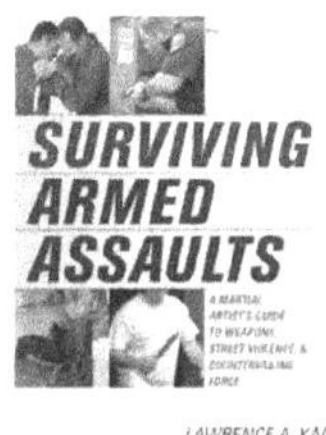

Surviving Armed Assaults (Kane)

"This book will be an invaluable resource for anyone walking the warrior's path, and anyone who is interested in this vital topic." – **Lt. Col. Dave Grossman**, Director, Warrior Science Group

A sad fact is that weapon-wielding thugs victimize 1,773,000 citizens every year in the United States alone. Even martial artists are not immune from this deadly threat. Consequently, self-defense training that does not consider the very real possibility of an armed attack is dangerously incomplete. You should be both mentally and physically prepared to deal with an unprovoked armed assault at any time. Preparation must be comprehensive enough to account for the plethora of pointy objects, blunt instruments, explosive devices, and deadly projectiles that someday could be used against you. This extensive book teaches proven survival skills that can keep you safe.

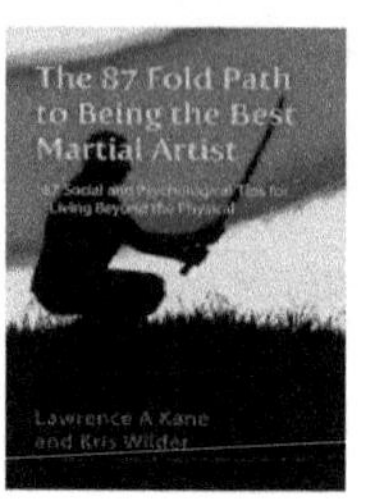

The 87-Fold Path to Being the Best Martial Artist (Kane/Wilder)

"The 87-Fold Path contains unexpected, concise blows to the head and heart... you don't have a chance, but to examine and retool your way of life." – **George Rohrer**, Executive and Purpose Coach, MBA, CPCC, PCC

Despite the fact that raw materials in feudal Japan were mediocre at best, bladesmiths used innovative techniques to forge some of the finest swords imaginable for their samurai overlords. The process of heating and folding the metal removed impurities, while shaping and strengthening the blades to perfection. The end result was strong yet supple, beautiful and deadly. As martial artists we utilize a similar process, forging our bodies through hard work, perseverance, and repetition. Knowing how to fight is important, clearly, yet if you do not find something larger than base violence attached your efforts it becomes unsustainable. *The 87-Fold Path* provides ideas for taking your training beyond the physical that are uniquely tailored for the elite martial artist.

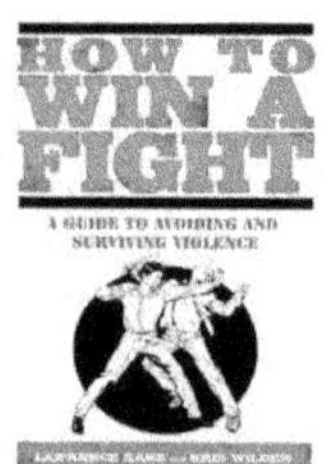

How to Win a Fight (Kane/Wilder)

"It is the ultimate course in self-defense and will help you survive and get through just about any violent situation or attack." – **Jeff Rivera**, bestselling author

More than 3,000,000 Americans are involved in a violent physical encounter every year. Develop the fortitude to walk away when you can and prevail when you must. Defense begins by scanning your environment, recognizing hazards and escape routes, and using verbal de-escalation to defuse tense situations. If a fight is unavoidable, the authors offer clear guidance for being the victor, along with advice on legal implications, including how to handle a police interview after the altercation.

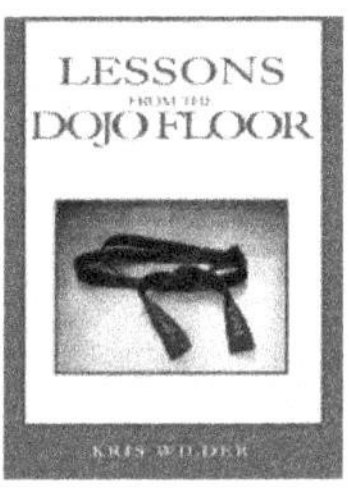

Lessons from the Dojo Floor (Wilder)

"Helps each reader, from white belt to black belt, look at and understand why he or she trains." – **Michael E. Odell**, Isshin-Ryu Northwest Okinawa Karate Association

In the vein of Dave Lowry, a thought provoking collection of short vignettes that entertains while it educates. Packed with straightforward, easy, and quick to read sections that range from profound to insightful to just plain amusing, anyone with an affinity for martial arts can benefit from this material. This book educates, entertains, and ultimately challenges every martial artist from beginner to black belt.

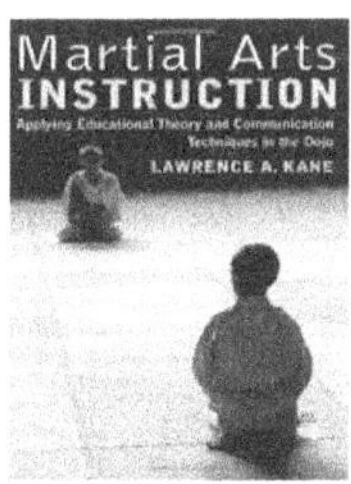

Martial Arts Instruction (Kane)

"Boeing trains hundreds of security officers, Kane's ideas will help us be more effective." – **Gregory A. Gwash**, Chief Security Officer, The Boeing Company

While the old adage, "those who can't do, teach," is not entirely true, all too often "those who can do" cannot teach effectively. This book is unique in that it offers a holistic approach to teaching martial arts; incorporating elements of educational theory and communication techniques typically overlooked in *budo* (warrior arts). Teachers will improve their abilities to motivate, educate, and retain students, while students interested in the martial arts will develop a better understanding of what instructional method best suits their needs.

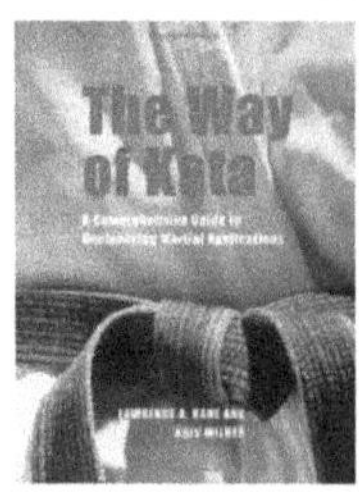

The Way of Kata (Kane/Wilder)

"This superb book is essential reading for all those who wish to understand the highly effective techniques, concepts, and strategies that the *kata* were created to record." – **Iain Abernethy**, British Combat Association Hall of Fame member

The ancient masters developed *kata*, or "formal exercises," as fault-tolerant methods to preserve their unique, combat-proven fighting systems. Unfortunately, they also deployed a two-track system of instruction where only the select inner circle that had gained a master's trust and respect would be taught the powerful hidden applications of *kata*. The theory of deciphering *kata* was once a great mystery revealed only to trusted disciples of the ancient masters in order to protect the secrets of their systems. Even today, while the basic movements of *kata* are widely known, the principles and rules for understanding *kata* applications are largely unknown. This groundbreaking book unveils these methods, not only teaching you how to analyze your *kata* to understand what it is trying to tell you, but also helping you to utilize your fighting techniques more effectively.

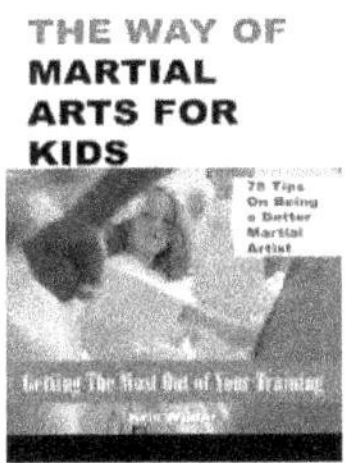

The Way of Martial Arts for Kids (Wilder)

“Written in a personable, engaging style that will appeal to kids and adults alike.” – **Laura Weller**, Guitarist, *The Green Pajamas*

Based on centuries of traditions, martial arts training can be a positive experience for kids. The book helps you and yours get the most out of every class. It shows how just about any child can become one of those few exemplary learners who excel in the training hall as well as in life. Written to children, it is also for parents as well. After all, while the martial arts instructor knows his art, no one knows his/her child better than the parent. Together you can help your child achieve just about anything... The advice provided is straightforward, easy to understand, and written with a child-reader in mind so that it can either be studied by the child and/or read together with the parent to assure solid results.

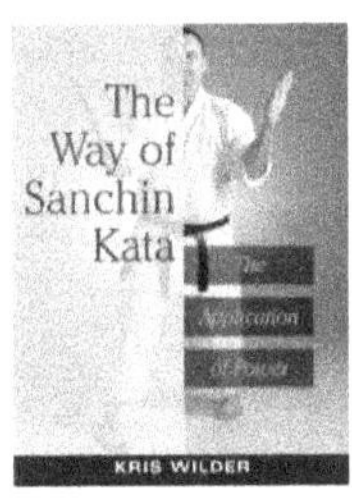

The Way of Sanchin Kata (Wilder)

“This book has been sorely needed for generations!” – **Philip Starr**, National Chairman, Yiliquan Martial Arts Association

When karate was first developed in Okinawa it was about using technique and extraordinary power to end a fight instantly. These old ways of generating remarkable power are still accessible, but they are purposefully hidden in *sanchin kata* for the truly dedicated to find. This book takes the practitioner to new depths of practice by breaking down the form piece-by-piece, body part by body part, so that the very foundation of the *kata* is revealed. Every chapter, concept, and application is accompanied by a "Test It" section, designed for you to explore and verify the *kata* for yourself. *Sanchin kata* really comes alive when you feel the thrill of having those hidden teachings speak to you across the ages through your body. Simply put, once you read this book and test what you have learned, your karate will never be the same.

Sensei Mentor Teacher Coach (Wilder/Kane)

"Finally a book that will actually move the needle in closing the leadership skills gap found in all aspects of our society." – **Dan Roberts**, CEO and President, Ouellette & Associates

Many books weave platitudes, promising the keys to success in leadership, secrets that will transform you into the great leader, the one. The fact of the matter is, however, that true leadership really isn't about you. It's about giving back, offering your best to others so that they can find the best in themselves. The methodologies in this book help you become the leader you were meant to be by bringing your goals and other peoples' needs together to create a powerful, combined vision. Learn how to access the deeper aspects of who you are, your unique qualities, and push them forward in actionable ways. Acquire this vital information and advance your leadership journey today.

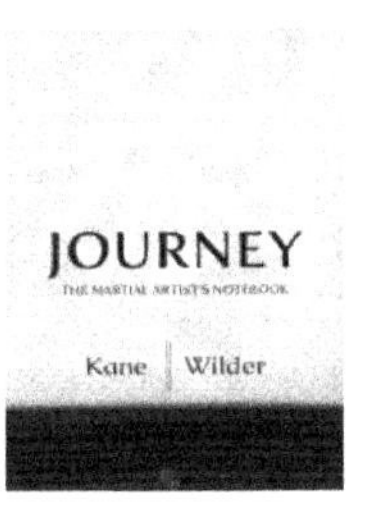

Journey: The Martial Artist's Notebook (Kane/Wilder)

"Students who take notes progress faster and enjoy a deeper understanding than those who don't. Period." – **Loren W. Christensen**, Martial Arts Masters Hall of Fame inductee

As martial arts students progress through the lower ranks it is extraordinarily useful for them to keep a record of what they have learned. The mere process of writing things down facilitates deeper understanding. This concept is so successful, in fact, that many schools require advanced students to complete a thesis or research project concurrent with testing for black belt rank, advancing the knowledge base of the organization while simultaneously clarifying and adding depth to each practitioner's understanding of his or her art. Just as Bruce Lee's notes and essays became *Tao of Jeet Kune Do*, perhaps someday your training journal will be published for the masses, but first and foremost this notebook is by you, for you. This is where the deeper journey on your martial path toward mastery begins.

The Way to Black Belt (Kane/Wilder)

"It is so good I wish I had written it myself." – **Hanshi Patrick McCarthy**, Director, International Ryukyu Karate Research Society

Cut to the very core of what it means to be successful in the martial arts. Earning a black belt can be the most rewarding experience of a lifetime, but getting there takes considerable planning. Whether your interests are in the classical styles of Asia or in today's Mixed Martial Arts (MMA), this book prepares you to meet every challenge. Whatever your age, whatever your gender, you will benefit from the wisdom of master martial artists around the globe, including Iain Abernethy, Dan Anderson, Loren Christensen, Jeff Cooper, Wim Demeere, Aaron Fields, Rory Miller, Martina Sprague, Phillip Starr, and many more, who share more than 300 years of combined training experience. Benefit from their guidance during your development into a first-class black belt.

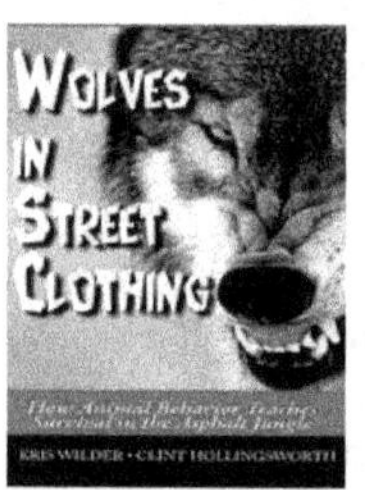

Wolves in Street Clothing (Wilder/ Hollingsworth)

"Teaches folks to rekindle tools that are already in us—already in our DNA—and have been there for thousands of years." - **Ron Jarvis**, Tracker, Outdoorsman, Self-Defense Instructor

This book gives you a new light in which to see human predatory behavior. As we move farther and farther from our roots insulating ourselves in technology and air conditioned homes we get disconnected from the inherent and innate aspects of understanding the precursors to violent behavior. Violence is not always emotionally bound, often and in the animal kingdom is simply a tool to access a needed resource—or to protect an essential resource. Distance, encroachment, and signals are keys to avoiding a predator. Why would a cougar attack a man after a bike ride? Why would a bear attack a man in a hot tub? Why would a thug rob one person and not another? The predatory animal mind holds many of the keys to the answer to these questions. Learn drills that will help you tune your focus and move through life safer and more aware of your surroundings.

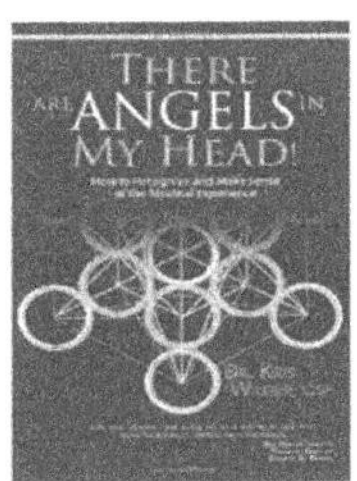

There are Angels in My Head! (Wilder)

"This is not a book on doctrine, dogma or collection of creeds to memorize in order to impress others with knowledge. This is a practical application of your participation in a new experience. Here you will find your questions answered even before they are asked." – **Br. Rich Atkinson**, Order of St. Francis

The unexplainable has happened. A prayer has been answered, a gift has been given, a communication has occurred... Is it the voice of God, or the voices in your head? Here's how to find out: In this groundbreaking book, you will discover the organization of the mystical experience. Based on the classic works of G. B Scaramelli, an 18th Century Jesuit Priest, Wilder brings modern relevance to any person to apply to their journey as they seek the Divine. Using examples and principles from Christianity and other religions, Wilder demonstrates that mankind's profound mystical experience crosses all cultures and religions.

Fiction Books:

Blinded by the Night
(Kane)

"Kane's expertise in matters of mayhem shines throughout." – **Steve Perry**, bestselling author

Richard Hayes is a Seattle cop. After 25 years on the force he thinks he knows everything there is to know about predators. Rapists, murderers, gang bangers, and child molesters are just another day at the office, yet commonplace criminals become the least of his problems when he goes hunting for a serial killer and runs into a real monster. The creature not only attacks him, but merely gets pissed off when he shoots it. In the head. Twice! Surviving that fight is only the beginning. Richard discovers that the vampire he destroyed was the ruler of an eldritch realm he never dreamed existed. By some archaic rule, having defeated the monster's sovereign in battle, Richard becomes their new king. When it comes to human predators, Richard is a seasoned veteran, yet with paranormal ones he is but a rookie. He must navigate a web of intrigue and survive long enough to discover how a regular guy can tangle with supernatural creatures and prevail.

Legends of the Masters
(Wilder/Kane)

"It is a series of (very) short stories teaching life lessons. I'm going to bring it out when my nephews are over at family dinners for good discussion starters. A fun read!" – **Angela Palmore**

Storytelling is an ancient form of communication that still resonates today. An engaging story told and retold shares a meaningful message that can be passed down through the generations. Take fables such as *The Boy Who Cried Wolf* or *The Tortoise and the Hare*, who hasn't learned a thing or two from these ancient tales? This book retools Aesop's lesser-known fables, reimagining them to meet the needs and interests of modern martial artists. Reflecting upon the wisdom of yesteryear in this new light will surely bring value for practitioners of the arts today.

DVDs:

121 Killer Appz (Wilder/Kane)

"Quick and brutal, the way karate is meant to be." – **Eric Parsons**, Founder, Karate for Life Foundation

You know the *kata*, now it is time for the applications. *Gekisai (dai ni)*, *Saifa*, *Seiyunchin*, *Seipai*, *Kururunfa*, *Suparinpei*, *Sanseiru*, *Shisochin*, and *Seisan kata* are covered. If you ever wondered what purpose a move from a *Goju Ryu* karate form was for, wonder no longer. This DVD contains no discussion, just a no-nonsense approach to one application after another. It illuminates your *kata* and stimulates deeper thought on determining your own applications from the *Goju Ryu* karate forms.

Sanchin Kata: Three Battles Karate Kata (Wilder)

"A cornucopia of martial arts knowledge." – **Shawn Kovacich**, endurance high-kicking world record holder (as certified by the Guinness Book of World Records)

A traditional training method for building karate power, *sanchin kata* is an ancient form. Some consider it the missing link between Chinese kung fu and Okinawan karate. This program breaks down the form piece by piece, body part by body part, so that the hidden details of the *kata* are revealed. This DVD complements the book *The Way of Sanchin Kata*, providing in-depth exploration of the form, with detailed instruction of the essential posture, linking the spine, generating power, and demonstration of the complete *kata*.

Scaling Force (Miller/Kane)

"Kane and Miller have been there, done that and have the t-shirt. And they're giving you their lessons learned without requiring you to pay the fee in blood they had to in order to learn them. That is priceless." – **M. Guthrie**, Federal Air Marshal

Conflict and violence cover a broad range of behaviors, from intimidation to murder, and they require an equally broad range of responses. A kind word will not resolve all situations, nor will wristlocks, punches, or even a gun. Miller and Kane explain and demonstrate the full range of options, from skillfully doing nothing to applying deadly force. You will learn to understand the limits of each type of force, when specific levels may be appropriate, the circumstances under which you may have to apply them, and the potential cost of your decision, legally and personally. If you do not know how to succeed at all six levels, there are situations in which you will have no appropriate options. That tends to end badly. This DVD complements the book *Scaling Force*.

Foreign Language Translations:

Instrucción En Artes Marciales

(Kane)

No es completamente cierto el dicho de que «los que no son buenos en la práctica son los que se dedican a la enseñanza». Sí es cierto, a veces, que quienes son buenos en la práctica no saben enseñar eficazmente. Este libro es único, ya que ofrece un enfoque holístico de la enseñanza de las artes marciales, incorporando elementos de la teoría educacional y técnicas de comunicación habitualmente pasadas por alto en budo. Es una obra que ayuda a los profesores a elevar su habilidad para mejorar la formación de sus alumnos, y donde los practicantes podrán desarrollar una mejor comprensión de qué métodos educativos se adaptan óptimamente a sus necesidades.

Vía Del Kata Sanchin

(Wilder)

El kata sanchin forma el núcleo desde el que irradian todos los demás katas. Su práctica lo guiará en el kata tal como fue concebido originariamente y descubrirá que es muy diferente de la forma moderna de kárate que hoy se suele practicar. El kata sanchin fracciona los movimientos según unos principios de progresividad cuya comprensión resulta imprescindible si se quieren adquirir las habilidades necesarias para dominar el arte de la mano vacía. Cada capítulo, concepto y aplicación se acompaña con una sección de "poniéndonos a prueba", diseñada para que el lector explore y verifique el kata por sí mismo. Los contenidos principales que se desarrollan en el libro son: movimiento no visto, la columna vertebral, la estructura energética, la camisa de hierro, la mente, la proporción 5:7, el kata tradicional íntegro en movimiento paso a paso, el paso de media luna, huesos-tendones-músculos, la estructura mecánica, el enraizamiento, el sanchin de diez minutos, entre otros.

日本の空手家も知らなかった　三戦(サンチン)の「

(Wilder)

空手が最初に沖縄で開発されたとき、それはすぐに戦いを終わらせるために技術と驚くべき力を使っについてでした。驚くべきパワーを発生するこれらの古い方法はまだアクセス可能ですが、彼らは意図的に見つけることが本当に専用のためのカタをサンチンに隠されています。カタの根幹が明らかにされるように本書では、身体の部分によって、フォームピース・バイ・ピース、身体の一部を分解することにより、実際の新しい深さに開業医をとります。すべての章、コンセプト、およびアプリケーションは、あなたが探検し、自分のためにカタを検証するために設計された、「それをテストする」セクションを伴っています。あなたはそれらの隠された教示は、あなたの体を介して経年あなたに話すことのスリルを感じるときサンチンのkataは本当に生きてきます。単にあなたがこの本を読んで、あなたが学んだことをテストしたら、あなたの空手は同じになることはありません、置きます.

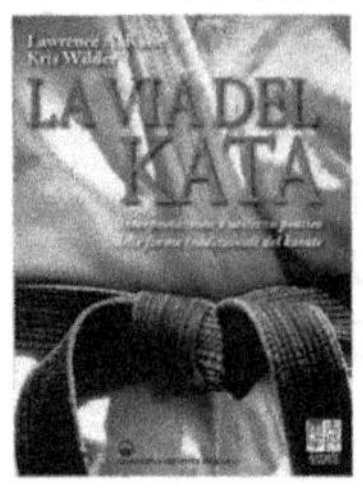

La Vía Del Kata
(Kane/Wilder)

Gli antichi maestri elaborarono i kata, o "esercizi formali", come metodi destinati a trasmettere i loro particolari sistemi di combattimento. Purtroppo essi svilupparono un sistema di istruzione a doppio registro, ove un "cerchio esterno" di allievi recepiva inconsapevolmente delle forme modificate nelle quali venivano omessi alcuni dettagli cruciali o principi rilevanti. Solo il selezionato "cerchio interno", che si era guadagnato la fiducia e il rispetto del maestro, avrebbe ricevuto l'insegnamento degli okuden waza, le potenti applicazioni riservate dei kata. La teoria capace di decifrare le applicazioni dei kata (kaisai no genri) in passato costituiva un grande mistero rivelato unicamente ai discepoli fidati degli antichi maestri, che in questo modo proteggevano i segreti dei loro sistemi. Anche oggi, pur essendo i movimenti fondamentali dei kata ampiamente noti, le applicazioni pratiche avanzate e le tecniche sofisticate restano spesso celate all'osservatore casuale. I principi e le regole per comprendere i kata sono ben poco conosciuti. Questo libro svela tali metodi, poiché non solo v'insegnerà ad analizzare il vostro kata per capire che cosa sta cercando di dirvi, ma vi aiuterà anche a fare uso delle vostre tecniche di combattimento in modo più efficace, tanto nell'autodifesa quanto nelle applicazioni agonistiche.

Acknowledgments

"Gratitude is not only the greatest of virtues, but the parent of all others."

– Cicero (106 BC – 43 BC)

Jackson Wilder took a punch in the face posing for our cover shot, but we know that he can handle it. The glove used in that picture was provided by Kensho International (www.kenshoint.com), our first choice in martial arts gear. Dave Davies, John Lytle, and Marc "Animal" MacYoung reviewed the draft manuscript, gave us discerning feedback, and helped improve the quality of this work. Thanks guys! Your insight is very much appreciated. Any residual imperfections are our own.

www.ingramcontent.com/pod-product-compliance
Lightning Source LLC
Chambersburg PA
CBHW051941090426
42741CB00008B/1221

9780692693490